TBROKEN
TRUST

TBROKENT
RUST

DECEIVED WAS THE TRAIT OF LOVE

CHEETAH DIAMOND

BROKEN TRUST
DECEIVED WAS THE TRAIT OF LOVE

iUniverse books may be ordered through booksellers or by contacting:

iUniverse
1663 Liberty Drive
Bloomington, IN 47403
www.iuniverse.com
1-800-Authors (1-800-288-4677)

ISBN: 978-1-5320-4598-1 (sc)
ISBN: 978-1-5320-4599-8 (e)

Print information available on the last page.

iUniverse rev. date: 04/03/2018

ARMY CONNECT....

It all started at 6:10 AM in the morning. Miracle received 12 restricted calls before she answered and started stating bible verses and saying a prayer from the holy book to the person on on the other end of the phone line.

The person hangs up. Miracle called SS thinking it was him who called from the restricted number. No answer. She is thinking, he might be layed up with a mego, she calls his phone back immediately, she realizes she dialed the wrong number so she hangs up.

The phone is ringing. Miracle answers, hello, someone called Timmy. Miracle replies, no I think I missed dialed your number, then hangs up. Ring Ring (*telepnone ringing*). She screams, HELLO! Didn't I tell you I missed dialed your number. The voice on the other end of the phone says, it's me Kimmie. I was on the bus earlier and you wanted my hairstylist number. Oh, girl, I thought you was this jerk calling my phone probably trying to get some knooki. Anyway Kimmie says, call 555-1117, then hung up. Wow! that was Kimmie big butt, fly ass. The shorty from the metro bus uptown, who gave me black beauty's number. I thought she was that dude Timmy calling back. Oh well, I said to myself, on on to the next one!

I was talking to baby sister,baby sister Lexzi. She was like Miracle you the best playa! you put these niggas in the circlez.

Phone rings. I look at the caller i.d., the call I was waiting on. Oh SS blowing up my line. I am like hahaha! I pick up, he says, hey Boo, come seee me. I say, sure. Why? he says, so I can beat it up! So I am like naw! i dont need no one to beat it up. He like, Oh yeah, well I need you to twirl on it and bounce. I say, I am there Boo! give me a 1 hour and 45 minutes. We hang up.

I arrived at the bus stop around where SS lives, he met me and we argued from the bus stop till I walked in the front door of his crib.

He was like nobody coming don't worry, we sexed
from the front room to the bathroom. When
I stopped, I took my piss and then the

floor to the bedroom toe the couch

then this white guy walked in my black ass was
like what is going on and SS says, he is

cool, he is my brother, he was in the Army with me. He
did turn out to be a good guy. I walked out the door of his
crib because I asumed the place was his brother and

he was on his break from the Army. He said
come back here because he thought I was

pregnant. Mind you he like, baby mother come here. I said, I had an abortion dude. He like, well I got kicked out the Army slim. I turned andwalked off trying to go to the bus stop. I came back seen SS sitting on the stoop with some fat dude so I sat behind them. The fat dude look back and said damn your

2

baby got big. I said, no this is my second son and mind u I am thinking in my head this that bitch nigga Sonny who broke my son arm in the telly. He had his baby momma drop him off to take me on a date and have the nerve to be drunk off the Remy.

I was in the shower getting ready to go to dinner and the moives with Sonny so in the meanwhile he was playing with my son. Sonny playing throwing Celo on the

bed and I here Celo screaming and I run out the bathroom to see why my son Celo was screaming. I asked him are you o.k. as I am looking I noticed his arm was broke the

bone was stuck out but the skin wasnt torn. I hurried up and called my Mom for a ride to the clinic asap! Sonnie kept trying to give me a couple of hundreds like it was hush money but I ran downstairs to meet my Mom and my Mom pulled up and I jumped in

the backseat with Celo. I could hear Sonnie screaming, Miracle, I am sorry. I do the same to my kids and they dont be get hurt. Well, this is not your child just remember. Sonnie and we pulled off. When I seen this nigga face again, I was disgusted.

Somebody came from behind SS and it lookeed like my cuzin. I said Sonnie is her name Roxi? and Sonnie said yeah. I said, Roxi u don't know your family! She said, Miracle! I ran gave her a hug and every body came out the house Vic and Shanee and

the kids of the corn.

I told Roxi I was having problems out of SS and she was like well fuck him up! How many times, I told Roxi I

didn't know who baby it was and I thought i was SS
baby and he mad and now sitting on the balcony.

Roxi and the family held Kazi and I went over
SS house. SS saying, Miracle don't

come over here with the bullshit. He climb up the balcony.
I am sorry I didnrt go to the army I am street train maybe if
it was a dog coming and a little ass gate. He was like, okay
come up the stairs and come in the door open i say okay spider
dancer. All I could think it was SS baby or the nigga who
kept blowing up my phone. Earlier when I was at home that
nigga was fancy, he made sure my hair was done, clothes, and
shoes fresh. He was my sugar daddy. He was a trick. When
SS left for the Army a little side money for Mircale had to be
made. Easy money, easy targets, lets getting bicthes! $250,

$300,and $600 wasn't no cheapster either. Big bottles of liquid. I
am stunting Miracle boyfriend Killer was in on all the schemes.
They were both trying to get high so ill get u. so as i walked in
to SS house we sat on the balcony and talked, thought about
how our baby would look, then he jumped off the balcony and
began to play football. I mean SS was the littles one. When i
mean word must have got around fast, it was like they tackled
his ass like a bean bag! His little ass flew like a plucked cigar.

MY TREASURED FRIEND

You were like a flower that bloomed from a seed
You were like my friend that had a smile like a daisy
We were like 2 stars that glistened in the night

4

We shined brighter than the moon
We attached like our unborn child
Ur tears were cold and bitter
We always knew how to make each other smile
We thought about sailing the seven seas
Until we made it to the city with no sorrow
We said we will always be there for each other
Through thick and thin
Through the stormy nights
Through the shallow winds
We fought together through the tough times
You always had a shoulder to lean on
Now I have no one to help me carry on
I will always remember our last words
Yet we were hard head and did what we did
People will never understand the pain we fill
To my best friend
God has open up his gates
That we had tried to sail to
Sometimes when we were on our own
The tears we cried was bitter and worn out
They flowed but took no form
We cried because our hearts was torn
And we found it hard to carry on
If I had one more time to see you
I would cry among my treasured friend
Who do you know that stops that long to help another to carry on
The world moves fast and it would rather pass us by
Than to see what makes us cry
It's painful and sad that sometimes when I cry no one cared about why
To my one and only true friend
From my heart to our soul
I will achieve all them again
I'll learn from my mistakes and try to achieve them again

But in my heart I know that I will never 4 get who is my true friend
There are no words to express how much I truly care
Just when I thought I d seen it all our paths crossed and
Met and I knew from the 1 sty glance you would be hard to forget
that smile

CHAPTER 1

KILLER RAPE

Miracle boyfriend sent niggas to Mircale or he talked about her goods. Number #1 rule never talk about your girl goods to the hood everyone goning to want to hit.

Chicken G rolled up on the bike, had a stack of money in his hand, talking about lets fuck. Miracle said boy get the fuck thats probably a bunch of ones, so Killer pulled down the same way Chicken G pulled up but chicken G pulled up threw the alley and Killer pulled up on the sidewalk. Killer starts screaming Bitch im gone kill u

Bitch! so Miracle runs around cars after cars from Killer. Stan said, man that girl aint bothering u Killer. Killer was like, she messing wit my family. Stan continued washing his car and telling Killer calm down, she aint messing wit ur family dude. Killer said, Miracle stand right there, im goning kill you and Killer rode his bike through the alley and Stan rode Miracle up the same way. Killer and Chicken G came and Miracle seen Mitts coming out the house and asked Mitts for a dipper. He said im going to the club ask my brother Sims for one, so Miracle ran in before killer came looking for her. When I went in the house, it was a party, it was 6 niggas chilling so I sat on the couch and waited patient and they took a long time, I should have known they was shcemeing on me. Sims gave me a triple stack louie vutton pill and 25 minutes later he gave me a dipper like What!it was wet to the tip and double dipped. I was so pressed I hit it in there. I thought I could pop the pill and moke the dipper and make it out there crib but when I hit the dipper on the side of there bed, I passed out, I don't even think i finished

the joint. I passed out on the bed. By time my head hit the bed my body was being tossed and turned and mouth going and them telling me they was recording it I was so gone I couldnt even lift my head. I got there at 12 p.m. they drag me out at 6 a.m. Before they drag me out I punch whatever nigga I seen. It was d i finally got my focus back a little, it was coming in an out. In my my head this nigga suppose to be my

friend, how could he sit there and watch it or fuck me out of my mind like that, so next thing I know I was on the next block getting whoopped by Killer, I didn't know it was Killer until 10 hits after. I was leaned on the car facing Killer and he just punching me all in my ribs and face. I could here voices, Miracle don't come back down here. I snapped up and I saw clearly it was Killer, I reached for my knife and stabbed him in the arm,

he backed up, then I saw his Aunt on the porch wit a bat and his cuzin behind two other cars wit a bat so I ran, I didnt know what was going on but this had to be a set up. I ran so fast in my brown cowboy heels and my little jean mini skirt and lovie vutton brown shirt with white letters on it. Killer was two steps away, he reached and grabbed my wig off my head and I kept running for bout 8 blocks, until I reached my house. I fell and tumbled all the way up my G-Ma stairs. G-Ma running to the door, what is wrong with you Miracle! I been raped and Killer beat me..

The next morning was the carribean festival. Me and my mom attended and left there walking to the police station. The police knew exactly who i was when I entered.

She was fucking killer she stepped from the desk called killer. and

killer called skit and like all 6 of them skited in me. i ran when killer called he said i heard u was at the police at the police station snitching. bitch im gone kill u. i told u i run this i know to many people.

I was still bleeding from my vagianl area and busted eye. I still here Killer shooting the

gun from last night when I ran off and out the police station.

that didnt stop me, I went home thinking I am going back again tommrow and my ribs was hurting, bleeding and I still wanting to go back. Looking inthe mirror, feeling bad I was raped and abuse all in 1 night. The next morning I went down to skitter place, that is what I called the block after the bullshit. Ran in to my cuzin Big Shot, he said Miracle, people on the block told me you flatten my tires last night. I say, no, I was beat and raped. He like, I dont care and you going to pay for my car or I am going to burn your little ass up! I said, okay do you. Then I saw Killer cousin and heard the Bitch put out a petition to get me locked up, talking about I done stabbed everybody tires on skitter place so now I am labled as crazy girl for what. I saw Killer walking out the alley, he like come on girlfriend

know my brother a police officer i said yeh ur girl is to.

how could this be word onthe street killers family took him to the hospital to get

stiched up. thats were

they decided to charge me wit a deadly weapon and destruction the police.i did 8 months and when

i pulled up from jail killer and his cuzin was in the alley talking and
they was the

snitches he was

so surprised. my dumb ass came right back to his ass. why i still
dont know.

He said tell you

LESSONS

little willow tree how bout thy
Sunshine on me and the little star of my life
Light thy on my soul so my tree top will grow further
East and west shallow winds
Sinking train, sink on me
Let me ride the plane or the train to destroy my sins
Get over our sinful life
Opium no more of the 7 years of my bad luck
Show me the light of success
Shine so bright on marriage doors
Open up for me to sail on my plain to the honey mooners
You know how I feel you I'm realistic as I can be
You called me fake cause we not ever knew ourselves
Fakeness of the planet of Venus
You was scared of me
I not ever thought I was goning to meet my match

I meet a man as physic therapy as he needs that means as well as you sail.

The drugs that affect the brains of the wise

There's no color of discrimination of telling lies or what lies beneath the streets

When you blow trees and that's what you first start to see and feel the baby movements of the heaven

Baby movements of the heavens God send me down blessings of survival lessons

But I intend to finish life with love not lust

Damage my soul lost books, I will find you and get you back

Worship my God and many blessings will be sent down to the earth in tune in me

CHAPTER 2

VIETNAM

right under ur parents noses and they wonder why mircale sees a doctor. miracle

was lost and greiving over her best friend kitten.who boyfriend was off the pilll and

dippers

and physco mentally ill. kitten and miracle went ever where together the three years

they

was together. messing wit big niggas getting money big drug dealers. at 12 threw 15.

it was like young girls gone wilder. believe me. kitten would talk to the niggas while

i still the stash. how cool is that. she was messing wit pat and i was messing wit loco

ken.

they both wa older than us. by 10 years or so we thought we was in love wit these

men

and it turn out to be a bad dream on the vitenam bricks. like one night i was sleep

this was before i met any body going to catholic school in the 8 th grade. my mommy

had a

2 bedroom and she was in there wit her dude name fiz.and i was sleepin and the bed

was by the

window and all od a sudden i felt someone rubbing my legs and my thighs and i

awoke and

scream and i ran in my moms room and fiz jumped up and ran out side and i seen the

dude

had on a black shirt and blue jeans. fiz seen a dude sitting out front at like 4 am. wit

the

same colors on. he swore he wasnt at the window. but was the only dude. Outside wow.

so the days went on of us living in vitenam. me and loren started going to highschool

at

vocational studies. and i had a fight wit a brad and meet loco ken and found a safe

in the apartment. so i began to seel drugs at 12 and hang wit the niggas i had

pumping at school. i gace up 2 onces aint know what i was doing just blessing people

so called loren and wakster lolo. every morning before i go to school i would roll up

wit

shawn he lived down mst ne. well me and him went to school high every morning.

as he got a little older became the top nouch drug dealer we began to distance

he began to beef wit pat. kittens boyfriend. so anyway me and loren wa walking

to the store and we seen t. he wanted loren and he said he was bringing a friend

for me

so i said no u can tell t wanted me i didnt want him doe. so later that night. t came

and

loco ken.thats how i met loco ken. they knocked on the door. we let them in. and

we went to

my room and loco ken i sat on his lap and loren was on my bed wit t. we left t and

loren in my

room. and me and loco ken went in my moms room. i just knew loren was bunking

that big ass over

for t.me and loco ken was in the other room talking alnight and they had to go cause

moms was

comimg home from work.

ever since then me and loco ken got distance. till i was standing in the hall and i seen

him going down

the stairs in the middle of the court and i said why u aint call me he said miracle u aint give me

ur number so i gave him my number and he said ill call so we talked
alnight alday and

moives

jelwery shoes late night talks and when birthdays came around cards
wit money. we

was scared to tell our

mothers we was talking cause he was older than me. so we sleep in
the car and then

he start sneaking me in

his moms apartment across the court my mom never new were i was
so. i felt like

she didnt care she was

o into fiz buying her all types of name brand purses and she was in
love wit the

money if u had it she new u.

any way i end chilling in the house one day while loco ken was down
davin house and

i sat at my moms

house listen to music. blasting u know how it was in the hood. so
t came and

knocked asking for loco ken.

and i said no hes not here he went to davin house and he said alright and i close the

dootr went back to

the big radio. and t came in ran on me grab me and held me led me to the leather

couch. holding

pushing me down. pulling my pants down fucking me raw. nutting all in me. i heard

the key i was so scared

i didnt want my mom to know what happen to me so i held the door while he

jumped out and open the door

my mom began to woop my ass. i began to cry cause i wanted to tell her. but i

couldnt so t start riding.

me wit him smokeing dippers wit me. so he was getting bitches. come to find out t

was loco ken sister

babyfather. and they was in it together fucking bitches. i was in it to get high now. so i was fucking

loco ken in the day and t at night. we was all hitting the telly together. loco ken

,t,miracle and t

bitches whoever t broght out to smash that night he would ask loco ken to switch

he would say no is u

crazy u aint fucking my girl. so me and ken sister end up cool at first and then loco

ken said they

wanted to talk to me and i said shited they aint trying to talk they trying to fight so

his sisters renee

and whitney was standing in the middle of the court and they had there three

friends one was pregnant

karla me and her dude and friends use to smoke together. so she was mad at me

shallow whale liked loco ken

and stifena was a tall brick. these bitches was trying to see me so my mom told me go down there ask them whats

good so i did as i was told. i said yah wanted me we all in the middle
of the court. and

renee talkinng behing her

big sis whitney and whitney was like 22 and renee was 15. and
screamn bitch my

mother dont want u calling

i was like well ur mom was just outside she aint say that. so renee
was like im gone

beat ur ass. so my mom was

ike take ur earings off and beat her ass. renee flew to the streets
talking big shit.

i walk down th 25 a steps left.

and walked up on her swinging this bitch was dropping every punch.
1,2,3,4,5,6, bam

she dropped. so

shallow whale and stifena grap my arms and and let renee get up
and get at me a

couple of hits. so karla

boyfriend runs up and graps these bigs bitches off me and then i
went for the

biggest on shallow whale

and im walking her down 1,2,3,4,5,6,7,8,9,10 till i got this bitch to the car wit my

elbow in her neck just

pounding her and while renee scared to touch me her and stifena. shallow whale

telling them get her off me.

so i let the bitch go and then i layed down to take a breather and whitney comes and

i heard somebody ssay

get up u know the whole hood was outside it was like 60 people watching. and here

come whitney. smashing me

in the face so my mom come behind her and smash her and then whitney and my

mom fighting and her mom

trying. to jump my mom. so i run to swing here come renee coming at me cause im

going to wards here mom since

they disrespectful. so me and renee back at it so t run up and loco ken running down the court steps.

t screamimg why u letting them fight he saying he didnt know he knew cause he

flew in the house when i

was approaching them. so me and my my let them go up the steps and everybody

was like that was the best

fight in a min. so we sat outside me and my moms they sat on they side across the

court we called my aunt punisher

and my god mother bullet proof. they balled up toting. saying what these bitches

want let them flex.

MENTAL

triple tales so far from my life
Tell me why I feel as though I sank so far
Now actually losing my life for so long
Losing my schooling my destination in my life
The course of woman and men.
Why we suppose to vote for are rights.
Strong and smart and pretty.
Woman that are lusting for mental and physical and sexual mistakes.
How far will you go for the show. will you make me the gift of light.
The walk of the burden that caught my family line.
Is not the curse it is broken.
They love the smile of the sunshine.
Show the rain running form the eyes of the star.
When the times cross the paths of the armor.
The song of the lonely homeless men.

You will began to light world.
Thy who praise the rain.
Will down pour the bleesings.
In the downpour.
And the rest of the surface.
I know the blew and the swell handy ment.
Odf the color of the snow.
The midst of the riding wit the police.
The race of the fun get you got you
I found the friend of the dreams and the acompanyof the dust.
The real estate of the minded heart of the pain the kindle sun.
The fire of the mionnight air.
Th eblues depths of the fear of the play your game right what was
dealt for you.

DADDY THE BOXER..........

punisher was my dad sister. and it all started when i was a baby.
momma
rose was gonna through misery dealing with my fathers death. daddy
shane was the
most lovable
person on earth. it was just dont croos him or his family or he will
break you off with
his bear hands.
all i knew as i was growing up was that he was stabbed in jail and
was about to be an
pro boxer.
im now above age and have and son name tez. my momname me
miracle. cause i
was just lucky.

to be born from an a man. who was so pround to help others. cause daddy shane
lost his life taking
up for a groan man. i would say im not mad that my father shane was taking up for
an man he
didnt know. i just wish he would have thought about me first. when i actually sat and
talk to daddy
shane mother momma white. my fathers mother. she sat in the kitchen after
cooking me a nice meal.
she lived on madison place terrance. she talk and told me the truth of the story of
daddy shanes death.
cause i wanted to here it out here mouth. we really didnt talk after several years. I
guess cause i looked like my

father. and when i glanced at my father picture in gma house he wore a purple boxer
shorts and boxing shoes.
withy his boxing gloves he was already a champ in my eyes. i could still remember
when i was a baby
and my daddy was holding me and they was snapping the pic of dadyshane and
auntie sue. he was holding me so

tight and proud. ghe he still holds my heart and i hold his heart. well gma white told
me daddy shane
was arreasted in an house for a drug charge. cause they was selling drugs in the

house. daddy shane was arrested
and was taking to lawren prison. waiting for a court date to be
realesed. while he
was in jail he was playing a
basketball game with some guys. and some jail mates got buck with
and man who
was innocent. daddy shane

didnt like people to pick on others who was innocent. so he approach
the seen and
talk to them thaey got reckless
and he wopped on at a time like six niggas on the court so he got
locked down in the
hole for two weeks.
later when the feds let my dad back out. they lead him back on the
unit. he watch
all oppents and
they watched him and by night time they was plotting to get shane.
so the six guys
had sent a inmate to the co
and told him well pay you if u let as split this nigga he says how
much. a g and some
work we have are peps will drop it off. so while shane was waitinf
rec to be over and
he fell asleep in the cell and his cell open and his cell was the
last to open so the other niggas
was out so they waited in the hall for the cell to open. so when it
did some niggas
was the watch out. and three ran

in all had blades man out of toothbrushes medal from the wall
sharpened down to a
blade. and bout time shane

had awaken. he was being stabbed in the chest stomach and all. so they ran back to
there cells to flush. the

weapons. and wash there hands so shane stagger to the the co. the same co who
got payed for this shit.
he watch as shane collasped to the floor so another co seen him drop so he called
back on the walkie talkie.
they helped him to medical carry him leading him to the strecther. the co going
crazy putting him on the
patio. exit him to the hospital. were he was in the emergency room bout time the
family got there and my mom

gma white daddy shane was taking his last breath.

now i know why momma rose was always putting me out the house. cause i was
startint to look more and more like

daddy shane. shane every passing day and hoilday i was put out. my fathers side
never really did to much for me

got rape when i was eight.
i had a lot of cuzins on my father side they were like my sister and brothers since i
didnt have any. as i grew up i

started to hate my raper. thats why i always protected my little cuzins cause i was abused sexually. anything they

needed me to fight for them i was there or scare so one off. all my cuzins was boxers
they hand swas register. i guess

they just wanted to protect there self call it boxer mania. family pros. auntie sherri
could barely stand me cause her

daughter melody use to lye on me constantly. melody left school one day and came
to my gma house to see me sfter

school and had some tree we went to the same school. so she must didnt see me
that day. and she ask me if i wanted

to roll up i said know. so she talk me in to smoking wit her and i broke it in half and
and walked her half way to

make sure she was ok and when she got home she told auntie sherri she got it from
me and it was hers and i just

broke it in half smoke my half and she smoke her half. sherri called me and blew my
ear of u smoke wit my

daughter gave her this drugs and i couldnt say nothing so i never smoke with melody
again. see auntie sherri

thought i started melody on drugs cause i was already labe of
smoking drugs but she
brought it to me. dame how

they do that. auntie sherri kept all her kids underneath of her. and
married sank she
took care of he was a good

man he took care of her kids and his the ones he inpregnanted her
with. he was fun
a mechanic. she loved him so

the family loved him.

OPIUM

Classes beats me tippy toes.
Grant me the slick shadows
Do me the release me from the trouble that starts to show.
This not a man worlds this is a woman word
I got you wiped like a paddle spanks my donkey.
Don't hide from the show offs.
Are you color blind or something.
Don't you know you crawl before you walk?
This situation about this marriage thing is upsetting to me.
Do I sit in the right paths?
The last chance.
A lover's lane of successful cheaters.
A one man army of love to these gang bangers.
Tell me how to invest my time in the one love thing.
Not the show girl thing.

More caress of the horrors of the pistil hissy pants brags.

Spent with our men who use our wet damp cherished map as a dip spot.

To get by in this game to get extra dope.

Show me protection you might be able to be my body guard.

You horror you can clean my feet.

Help me to be in control of my life you cried because they gave me hugs and kisses.

So you pulled our pants down to show off that hair Lester.

Choose me you showoff even in my hard times.

Gutter or lay down in the streams.

I choose my higher power.

I choose the raise of the life.

I seen you and you not gon get me you put this skuul on me.

And you played dirty and I hard wit the personal attendents.

And thy gave me the cross of the hand.

Soon I will be there and the floor will get the same affect in the.

I got the fame in the last days.

And in the end you will see defeat and th esoorow of the lame.

You wil not fight me I will defeat you.

You will not be the geust of the wrath of the.

Same life in the life after the time you got th e problem fix it layed in the.

Day and the night of the same in the one way corner store.

meet the enemy........
lats night john wanted to meet up wit me. our destintanation was to meet at the
subway

stastion. i called john from the pay phone. to see were he was. bout time i got to
rockcreek place to get momma rose

car. i took the car after i had just got back in the house from being put out. for bout a
week cause of the outragous

war that was going on between johns family and the whites my family. well john
never made it i guess he had

something else to do. while my little cuzins had lice in her blood stream. i had moved
in with john when my other

cuzin was moving out she was messing with johns cuzin. he was in jail for some
accident. well anyway i had stepped

onthe concrete not knowing it was wet and had to clean all the shit off my shoes and
i was bending down wiping

my shoe wit a napkin i had in my pocket book and john rode up on his bike behind
me and slap my ass. i said

dame u scared me i didnt think u was coming. bout time i bent back down i got back
up from wiping my shoe john

was gone i thought john was trying to get me back up the way to get me jumped
. john is killer john is his real

name. i staerted the cadi and pushed down johns house. why when he infected my pussy. but he aint to blame i let

him fuck raw. knowing and seeing were he came from. he made me have an fishy
ordor for about 5 months i guess

it was from him trying to get me pregnant and it wasnt fitting my body. i was so
happy that john had used a

condom one day cause after i looked in the condom it looked like roach scales. like
what was in the sopa dish. at his

house. i liked john not for were he was at. for him being him i understand that shit
happens and housing cost and a

remolded is even more. cause my gma house wasnt up to date neither we was in
the same position. when i had

might killer i had just waked up to get a bag and he had it and i gave him 15 and i
went to talk to my cuzins

drought and i explain to him i just coped from him and killer had spoke to me befor i
coped hey miracle and i sai d

hi and ask my cuzin how he know my name and tell him im trying to holla so he called
his phone and told killer

that i was trying to holla and he said tell her to come her so i walk
towards him and
he said u drink and popped to

trunk and pulled out some hot ass hendew and i said naw and he
said sit in the car im
bout to pull off let me get this

off \real quick and when he finish we spend off and went to drought
house he
nebver came so i told killer to get me

a dipper. and he said no and i said yes and we argued for about and
hour. and he
finally took me cause drought

never showed up. so then he said i will never buy u another one and
then we went
to his house. and
we did it like they call me a miracle.

me and john started to stay at is aunt house constanyly. until one
day john and me
went to get low that was his

right hand man and then we rode alway over se.. to get one of those
wet sticks and
then on the ride back john was

talking to me u fucking for sticks and i saming no im not. and low
was in the back
laughing and i saying i pay for

the shit i buy. so the feds was across the other side of the street and was pulling
someone else. so they was occupied.
i swevered the wheel. and we crash and john grab the wheel and swervered off and i
jumped out with the stash and

ran over the other half of the bridge. he called my phone i hit vitenam to this. dike
brad that john didnt like.

cause tor was fighting over me she wanting me and john disliked it. and i smoove
. went to her house rolled up for

bout three days. and i heard john car riding around vitenam alnight long. crit crit crit
creeping cause the wheel

was messed up. so when i popped back up home to killer house. i wasnt allowed in
the house i was wonder why cause

low told his aunt what happen to the car. i always swevered the wheelwe never
crashed never say never i guess

so. now we was at hotels everynight of the hour and the moives and resturants.
enjoying life.

so it was around christmas and john slut he messed wit before me the one the
whole neighbor hood hit there mascot.

name dreaonna called me told me john was in the car with a brad. see she was
probably mad she wasnt in the pic

so she was snitching and i was out md and jumped on the subway
hit two trains and
in up uptown. quick it was the

last train i ran to this nigga house to vatch this brad i knocked on
the door and i he
came and said hey and what

are u doing here miracle i thought u was at home. i said dreaonna
called me and told
me u was having company

were she at so i walked in looked around. and seen no one. and i
said oh she scared
u\
and u droped the bitch off. hole

time. i spent the night and went no were. and the same night we
went out back to
check th ecar thats were thet

stash was and the gun. whole time the stash was missing the gun
was missing the
back window was busted and it was

a mystery to be found out so u know who was on duty investergator
john cuzin janel
and she was the hood watch.

she had her own programs and it was to tell the police the whole nine and 411.

so some weeks went passed and low was over se and my cuzins bricks was living
over there andu know the neighbor

hood talks so. someone had just brought a gun and. so bricks was like let me see it
and he said this look like my man

joint and he said forreal. and bricks called john said man i think i found ur joint so
bricks ask shawty who sold u

this he said this nigga name low and he said oh low that thatg bitch ass nigga. so john
said my right had nigga
robb me. dame so thats how the window car robbery happen. so now they
approach low later on that night bout

time it was block time and he was out side everyday like he didnt know who robbed
his man and aint that a

bitch. as time went on it became valintimesday and every one was in the alley and
all the raga muffins was in the

alley and i trying to get something out of killer u know him gtiving money to a girl is
out the question now

providing he will the supply and i kept asking for money to get my nails done so he
gave me 40 dollars after his

men got on him so i can get my nails i stepped off to get my nails down down the ave
and guesss who was on the bike

coming to see if i really went to get my nails done killer. so as i finish we walked back
down the block.

i felt like i started a fashion in this alley. i had to many name brand purses and no one
elsedid so i thought i was

poor but everone has there own opionion about people u dontr see ur self and
others look in. all i know it was to

many black people in one spot. that car was the mascot the whole hood too turns
sitting in it getting high john den

brought another car a white 4 door hootie i coped that one and drove it most of the
time. cause that saturun macoy

was done that car was bullet proof so much stuff happen to the car. i mean it started
fights the girls in the hood

wanted to fight me and that was the word on the street. so dreaonna was john sex partner before me and i was his

woman if u asked me cause i wa always around he picked me up i
lived in there in his
bed no other and dreaonna

was walking to cvs to get her gma some meds so she asked me to
walk and bout
time she came out the store. a blue

hootie poulled up. it was a brad and her mother and she jumped out
the passenger
side talking to dreaonna saying

were miracl and i had my name on my arm miracle big ass day so i
said nothing just
showing my name. so she

taling to dreaonna and me listening her name was trish and her
mom so i said since i
had my son i will meet u in

the alley and she said oh and i said yeh ill see u. i went an approached
john soon as i
heit the alley and i said u

going round telling bitches i fucked up ur car whats between us is
our business and
he said my uncle told them

somebody else always tell them somthing ur aunt said i cant come
in cause ur car
and now ur uncle trying to get

me jumped. i said. know u den this shit. he said go wopp her talking
bout dreaonna
an di said ill be back and
i called my uncle drew and he pulled up and i let my sit in the car
he said come on
miracle and his friend watched

my son. and we knocked on the door and dreaonna gma open the
door and i ask for
dreaonna i siad dreaonna u
wanna smoke she came out stole her she drop and i stopped her and
i spoke to her
and bitch dont u ever try to get

me jumped. and stepped off cause her gma watched her grandaughter
get stopped
and i bucked at her and she

slam the door saying get in here dreaonna messing with these people
and i waiting
for trish and not ever seen trish.

word made it around. properly. thank you.

CHANGE IN MYSELF

This is my hypoventilation that got me moving slow and quickly.
The demons that made me fill so ill gotten.
The injection of the lord's sprit.
The klaxon of the devils people.
It's ok to laggard in the school.

The brain is like a kettle drum.
Some people are so insular with the word.
The education of the diploma will.
Have you iridescent in public.
You must be genial in school progress.
You may not groin in the teachers area.
The hoodoo of the devil will tell u to dropout.
You may founder May times keep going.
People may think our not frivolous in what u do.
You must hanker a good mind and pray.
And you all will receive.
People left the fame and the last days of the criminals.
Soak in the pain and the last not I will be there in the rest of the short maze and the.
Doers of the jester and fight for the lonely.
Find the sinners in the orifice.
Straight hard and the lessons of the son of the man
Did you find the mind frame of the season.
My mine is the devasted world wind in the paint.
Soon in the days will win in the corner in the maze.
Poker not the face at me you will not be in the same maze in the rupture.

back to the trap.....
so one night me and killer was together. we had spent the night in the trap house it
was some

ellaigant white folk and his black girl friend that was on coke hard but she was getting
it stayed fly and had big

shit and money. so i had on some baby blue draws and top to match the spaghetti string top looking oh so good so

me and killer got to arguing about thebrad dreanna and got to
tussling and he ran so
the white man tom came to

me trying to brake it up and i swung at tom like three times for
intervenning and
killer ran from me cause i was

off the boat and he was very ferious for me swinging at him and the
man who let us
stay in his house. so when killer

ran out tom house the police was outside and thought he had did
something so i ran
after killer when i put my clothes. And couldn't find
him to the next day. i walked down to killer from my house the next
morning and he
was standing on the block

hustling and he seen me and just stood and there looking at me like
i was a bad vibe
. so he said i aint fucking with u

no more. i said oh yeh and left so. the next day i called killer phone
and a guy had
answered and he said he dont

want to talk he said u crazy. ur the crazy girl. so he was trying to
holla so my gma had
just got an new alarm

system and i couldnt get out cause i didnt know the code. so he came his name was
skip cause we skiped killer out the

picture. when could only see each others faces and the next day he came he
brought some money to get my hair

done in some senegalese i was so amazed at this guy he was caramel red and was a
money making got on the strip

and had a brain as a writer. so we kept talking i was out back of nmy gma house and i
heard a little boy on the

phone i said who baby u got and my gma came to the back door and said come here
and i was steady goning on

skip so i came in the house and skip was on the front porch wit my son and putting
some tennis on his feet the new

harach shoes. so then he had brought him some to and i was like were mines at he
said i got ur hair done. i was so

happy then when he left i went to go see killer and was so high. i was sitting on killer
lap. and skip and his man

drew walked up and said if u dont get off that nigga lap im finish wit u. so i never

45

moved. me and skip remain

friends he still gave me half onces of juice and it was fine.

WHO I ADMIRED

The geodesy is the devils wrath.
God left him here.
He was thrown out the clouds to the earth.
God made equinox so we would shine.
He died on the cross for our sins.
The heaven gates have a flamboyant.
The atmosphere of the devils earth smells like feta.
The lord will bring from between the fjord.
He will make woman like an empress.
Things seem so fitful now on the earth
There battling like beats for their life.
The devils make it seem like your sins are flunk and its wrong.
The lord flagellate is so fierce you will fall and bow to him.
Yes it wasthy who I admire I seen you from far away.
I made the way out of the day I went to the.
I made the real chance of the last dots of the foreign company.
Kind and the made mission you gave me to survive
I was just hoping I didn't die like the old sir.
Done in the same name and the players in the fine arts.
Plunder the waist in the down right.
Madness of the getting the best out of the mind and surviving in
the tables.
You made you I made the mess and scoped it in the bush.
You made the trouble and the same day I made the crime.
You say the lame in the finally and the raven in the yesterdays paper.

This talk is the talk of the town and the gossip in the.

adopting from hell......
my little cuzins was about 4 years old and she met a friend at school
that would come

around and house spend a nights and as the year went on her father
killed her
mother. he stabbed her 56 times. in

front of her and her two brothers. so the aunt had cancer and so my
uncle took in
the two youngest kids. sasha and

gus. and the oldest one went to his other family his girls house. they
were already
kinda of messed up in the haed

baecause the father did that in front of them. so now he got locked
up for the rest of
his lie 50 or better years. so as

time passed little sasha had and behaivor problem like there evil
child. she was so
good at her intelligenece. she

would turn everyone agaisnt the person as a child. as she got older
she even broke
my uncle and his wife up made

there life and living hell and when my uncle sent her down dc to
live wit my gma and
i was accused of everthing

she did.. like we had went down to my gpas funneral and my grandad thought i had
something to do with the

missing camera and i took the the pics with his camera and why would i still the
camera and i was the
room door and i dont even smoke weed she sexed my boyfriend and meet him at
the waterpark with a friend for his

friend. no one believed me about her ways she was agaisnt me and acting like she
was my family like demail of her

intentions to ruin someones life and she told me after she got me in trouble and i
was getting put out that maybe it

was meant for u to leave u be better far away from them. adopting from hell she
almost got my cuzins locked up

cuz she probably was flanting pass him she end up going to high school meeting the
wrong crowd and a dike and

ran into trouble she ran away so much wit the dike. and one day never came back
and meet a pimp so they turn

her papers in to sent to foster care. cause they couldnt handle her espeaically her
tricking i mean i see she was well

taking care of clothes trips nice eatersand all. she took my killer.
she thought.

WHERE I WANT TO BE IN
A COUPLE OF YEARS

I want to move in diverge life.
I want to be in a dove cote and fly when ready.
I want to have money like a douse.
They gone been dumbfound at the fame of m
The lord will down pour all my blessings.
I will devein many people like god told me.
He will dotty those whom go to the devil materials for fun and the
desires.
I will always give doxogyl for you to praise god.
We will become unblock to Jesus family.
Which will make us like him.
Kindle I on the first machine in the first way I meant the day.
You saw the dream far before cause you seen the death of the lord
I brought back
And thy will sing joyous songs of the seasons,.
I seen the letter I wrote and the finally.
No one will be the feather in the loss ones in the name of the famous.
I will pay the day in the fundamental war.
Pay no tension to the promises.
While in the mention in the bests of the random pain.
You are the lessons of the loner.

liked by ur wounder.....

so after killer and skip was aressted for selling drugs a new crew came around and
has

moved in the rooming homes. so i meet chris, and simon. they were nice and chris
would always by me some

cigaretts and a drink. like a cooler i didnt drink anything hard. miracle liked sweet
things. and so chris new i was

into killer and killer was into me. so he still tryed his hand and i still would not give
cause it wasnt right that

everyone in the neighboorhood wanted to fuck miracle. so as time went on miracle
kept seein chris. he was way pissy

drunk and he was out of control trying to get on top of me and kiss me i tryed to
push him off and then i began to

try to kick him. he finally got off of me. and when i tryed to exit the room he hug me
and i had a knife on my was

he grabbed it and stuck miracle in her back. and miracle looked like what why and
tryed to grabbed the knife so

he wouldnt stabbed her constantly. so them ended up in the hallway of the roomimg house. chris and miracle was

tussling for the knife blood was running across the wall like a straight line like 3 rulers
long. and miracle began to

knock on a door taking his hand and hers. and the people in the rooming house
began to hear the noise. so the open

there doors and one old man open it and closed it and the guy from the basement
room looked and closed there

door they probably new him and aint want to be a snitch and they were on his side
. so chris went in the room and

just looked in the hallway from the room. and miracle said give me my purse and he
stood and gave her the purse.

so miracle left and walked up the street mad. walked all the way from 13 st to kdy on
the way there she meet a guy

and he took her in to clean the wound it was a party going on and she didnt want to
put the achool on the wound so

she left cause she didnt want them to call the ambulance so she hit kdy and sat at
the bus stop and a spanish gtuy

said u need to go to the hosiptal to get it stitched. so miracle called the ambulance. when they came they took

miracle to the hosptal asking her his name the police investigator.
so she felt like i
had an attidude and left miracle

was in pain and she was getting stitched up why would u come in
and ask any
question while a person is getting

stitched up miracle thought so they dropped the case so she felt it
was good miracle
got stabbed. oh lucky chris.

What Will The World
Be Without You?

There would have no purpose.
I would be constraint to the trees and animal.
It would be no cult.
There would have been no cult.
There would have been no culpable.
Punishment for Lucifer and his angels.
We would have not ever used crampon to get the lord.
My darling I always knew you was an purpose in my life
That's why he sent you to me threw someone else
Even it was threw a friend.
He made that happen.
Realize the love we have.

The world would be lost with out a lady like m e.
The submission I feel the need.
To climb on the pahs an dliv ein the same singer.
That gave you up and made you the most for the same.
This is the mentio time to shine and not ever loose your shine.
I made th eprosmise to my god to see the future an d live and long
divine life.
I ought to dream in the same way in th e past was in the foreign
ways.
I not the funny mustard in the likeable time.
Housing me weas easy what took you so long.
I made th e issue in the natraul air of the ran ning down.

war between love n envy.....
there was astrong black intelligent boy talented boy his name was
wayne. he was
raised in a caltholic school. he

finished in an public school and was the star football player.
constantly i told him
when he finish dont run the

streets. he had seen me wit this guy that had worked at fed h supplies
and he said he
wanted to go apply mine u

wayne was my little cuzin. he would sit underneath me talk alnight
play fight. he was a
boxer like my dad shane.

shane was his uncle but they never met.

it just runs in the family line to box. he had moved out of gma whites
house and

found a girl wit her own place. he

would tell me to come around and i was but i was on my get high
shit. i was smoking
and chasing the monkey. so i

end up going to my uncles clubme and killer and met up wit the
rest of the whites on
my father side since that was

my father last name. they called waynes father the bosshe had the
greatest bond
with aunt sofe and she was

patrolling the door while my dude parked my cheerkic truck. i
waited at the entrance
wit my cuzins.

so the boss popped the ed harvy drink it was 150 a bottle and we
loved. a nice night
on the town. so me and killer

danced and took a break at the same time and every family member
who smoke
took a break on the patio to chill

and reminicse. lilwayne saw on the patio and came to me and pulled
a bag oout his
crouch of his pants and said u

trying to buy this i started to laugh me and killer cause that was my
little cuzins and it
was funny cuz why is it

down there and he took some backwoods and rolled up his own supply cause me
and killer smoke weed on ocassion

and we definitly was not taking weed from my little cuzin. i still seen wayne as a little
boy when he moved out

because i can remember him around as a child little partys not be boy partys like the
club.
im just wondering why they let him move out

so me and my dude went home and did the do alnight long. me and killer was like
cake and iceing i was the cake

and he was the icing. well wayne was interested in this girl and spent every moment
with her. i guess she thought she

was the one. maybe in the beginning she tryed to be two faced and play to dudes at
the same time. on e from se and

the other from upt that was wayne upt so were wayne hung at upt he began to
befriend the dude inthe neighboe

hood. him and his cuzinz choas his father was a big rapper so niggas was hating on
them 24/ 7 trying hit the hit to

them and some just wanted to be ass kisser. they stuck together like twist since kids.
cusinz and bestfriends. they down

14 st area together. they began to look hot because they were so fasionable. as
niggas. as niggas began to wonder

were they was pulling this money from for shoes and clothes. they say young and fly
who these cats. well choas grew

up around 14 st they began to express there feelings and experiment with guns u
know they sayin live by die

by. wayne had brought a duece duece.

the word was that wayne was robbing people up the way between his new hirl and
the streets was a bad business

deal. she began to flirt with both dudes wayne and the nigga over se. this bitch was
an mischeif and she ended up

pregnant and told both of them that they was the father. wayne was just at the
hosiptal with his sister baby and

her babyfether who would have known he had one on he way u miracle be
everywhere so i was there when cassidy

had the baby. cassiddy look just like wayne just was a girl. wayne
was a good brother
to not leave cassiddy side well

she had birth. he sat there for three days. he held little contour tightly
thats his first
neice. days went passed and no

on heard from wayne in four days.

ring ring the phones rings it the morgue in b more careful md
they called choas house and spoke to his gma and said can u come
adentify this
body the person has a name on the

arm of w. sh e said wayne no it couldnt be. she hurryed up an dcalled
the bossand

sofa and they got there brother max to ride and they were so
emontional the boss son. u
know they made a big mistake

messing with the boss son. so they rode for about and hour and
pulled up to an big
hospital looking like and

haunting house. they went in and veiwed the body and saw wayne.
laying on the
morgue telling he could have

passed out. and he was hsyterical and so blue.
bout time they had the funneral it was arguements and was it the
baby of wayne
and the funneral came around

so fast it had to be like 300 people there they were sitting in balcony. and the girl
popped up with her pregnant

belly and began to approach wayne father at the casket and the boss said nothing
he was just in shallow tears and

sofe and her daughter led her her out the church with her mischeif ass they wouldn't
show miracle who she was they

just made her leave cause they new miracle was in the game hard she would have
swung. the reason they exited her

cause they thought she had something to do with waynes death and the word was
the guys who was around 14 st

had drove hime over se were his so called baby mother be on 51 st se. how they
just end up on the same street well

they pulled in the alley and the driver hoped out and the passenger cause the driver
friend was in the car and

wayne got and the driver was like it ur baby naw its mines and they new wayne
could fight like to well so his only

option was not to use hands and he pulled out the gun the driver and his friend was like no and he busted like 10

tomes and pulled off wit his man see that why they wouldnt allow her in the
funneral she wanted to tell the boss

that. that was waynes baby. the boss could have trangled that girl by the casket. I
would have so rip wayne.

EXPLAIN OUR WORST AND OUR BEST

I'm a concubine to Jesus.
An adagio in the heaven.
You are no worthy of benighted life on the earth.
You are adroit to him in many ways.
You are a berk you the demons.
He made you a ragged.
God makes you bibliophile to open our eyes.
You need to admire god.
He makes to admire god.
He makes u have bonny body.
The devil will make our mind wonder and hallucinate.
I'm an acolyte.
He knows u sin.
He died for our sins.
He tells you to repent.
He tells you come follow him.
He doesn't tell you to be atrophic in heaven.
You will have no fear of earth.

Thy will hate on thy past and thy sunshine wont mater in the past
You swine the mission.
I see the program in the likeable.
Ways in the same made you join the lamer.
I seen the rest of the label and they made the fame in the seen.
I mea n you was the finer golds that made you
smile at me in the next life I mean the rest of the days
you was name the kin.
Love the maze in the ink in the tame er I was
lost in the main room in the polished area

Valentimes Mistake........

onece apon a time there was a girl name miracle as u know and a
the brad name
dreanna and miracle pulled up

to the back of killer house and killer was coming out the house and
dreanna and killer
cuzinzso i approached killer

why she coming out ur house just fucking killer my friend said in
her truck and lead
killer to the side pulling out the

knife and he bang my head into the parking pole and u know that
he was fucking
that bitch. if he puts his girl

head into the pole and i looked back his aunt was in the back of me
and i went to the

car and went to get my uncle

luke an wayne before he died and uncle rollin.
me and wayne was on the side walk
and uncle luke was in the house

and uncle rolling was in the house getting a golf club we was laughing
luike were the
guns at and i heard that a

golf club will kill u and uncle luke was like he will meet us down
there so me and my
destiny was in the car and we

went to pick up three other brads just in case. so bout time we got
down there my
uncles pulled up it was three cars

all together. uncle luke and his four friends wit there pistols and
uncle rollin wit his
golf club. so we seen my other

cuzin wit his babymother and ask weres killer and they said i dont
know so we
walked around looking for him and

we seen like 15 niggas on the block and was like were he at and no
one reply then
we got he aint here they no we

had work. see dreanna wanted to fuck both of us she would pop my
draws and i
knew she been down there before

and he was fucking her cause she knew how to turn the tv off and the radio unless it
was really before me. u know me and killer made up the same night. we went to the
hotel in md and layed up and he called me dreanna i swear it let the devil out of me i
was aiming lamps, ash trash and throwing his clothes over th ebalcony and then he
threw mines and why would we do that he says miracle u better get ur clothes
cause im not getting it and he ran i ran necked to get my clothes as vice versa him
getting his so we went to themall to play pool and get something to eat and he gave
me the money for my food so i seen a shoe store and coped a pair of shoes and he
didnt like that u know the saying buy a woman a pair of shoes they will walk out ur
life and so killer threw my shoes in the water fountain at the mall and flew up the
stairs and how bout two niggas ran for the shoe sand one jumped i mean too nd one
actually got them and was he blue in the face looking stupid. on valentimes day.

HE WILL NOT FORGET YOU

God will bless you so much
You will bequeath your love ones.
You won't need acupressure in heaven.
You won't need a bed fellow in heaven.

You will be at rest and in harmony.
The devil will leave you at your own will.
He will Adulation your mind and makes you ill.
So you won't succeed.
Fight it get on our knees.
Pray with a group and by yourself.
Let him know who you are finding who he is.
Cherish the time you spend reading his word.
This is the gelian to the lord.
You're not a bark be wise.
Get our humiliation.
Don't fear your goals.
Jerk it out to succeed.
Pretigous you made me thought I was the
duck that ran in mud you flamed in the.
thy shotter in the same wind in the person of the license in th e
in the lame r I fought the dinner in the next life
not starvation I sit in the shallow winds.
why not starv in the present seen my hand was left in the.
Kindness for the weak ness for the past tense for the next time you
seem to vegan
Its good you can do any tryable thing you cjhoose to do.

BECAREFUL WHOM U SLEEP WITH....

well when i was young it was a guy name standley and he wold
always watch me as a
child around about 12 and
he would say he was going to get me and and i didnt even know
him a friend that
stayed around the corner from

my gma house was saying stay away from him he skitszode. and as
i grew i finally
went and talk to him we smoke

ther the water together and booked brads together. and finallly i
was on the hill and
i wasdaty a dude out mo

county and the last stop was standley house so i did want a baby
thats why i slept
with bruno, ken and stanley and

it wasnt meant top happen wit standly and ken had just gave me a
bottle of h20 and
i smoked all night wit stanley

and bruno was my boyfriend and i just broke up wit him but bruno
thought i was
pregnant by him so did ken i

thought it was bruno but so happen it was the last nut i know it
sounds nasty i was
young and dumb. and i end up

getting locked up in juve and and did 8 months and the last month
of my pregnancy
was at home wit bruno cause he

stuck it out wit me and when the baby came out he was red like stan
and boy the
brads on the blocking was geeking

to see the pic. when they seen the pic they said thats stan baby and
i real i said u

think so. the perral sisters was like

yeh. and if so i sure was so i seen stan like two months later after i
had tez and when
i seen him he was wit kobby

and chesse and i caught up to them on the way to the store and when
we made it to
the store talking and and he seen

some friends of his and it was a dude and a his girlfriend. i didnt
know them never
seen them before so we all walked

back to the block i said stand let me take this back to this bread to
my gma. and he
said ok. so bout time i came

back outside i seen kobby and cheese sittting on kobby porch and i
said were stand
and they started to laugh and i

was like what so funny stop playing were is he. they replyed in the
alley on his back
porch. so i went and seen them

smoking and i said let me hit it and he replyed u dont want to hit
this and the guy
girlfriend said u know i dont like

u doing that and i said what is it i seen the pipe and started to cry
and it didnt matter
but he was my babyfather

my rep. i wasnt meaning to let him be my babyfather,. it just happen and stike two
my gma put me out for

something and i was homeless and i met a dude i was coming from school and he
was dressed northface jordans and
all so i wouldnt have thought anything other he came around smoking weed and i
begane to like him and i know i

need to lay my head at times i was locked out the whites home after my moms side
put me out and u know

sometimes u got to do what u do. well miracle had 7 abortions cause her mom made
her have them young cause she

felt miracle was to young to take care of a child so miracle in up getting pregnant on
valintimes day by the

northface nigga i thought his name was nick and my little cuzin was telling who
nobody name nick and then they

said slick i just knew they didnt know him they said slick and he smoke butter and
come to find out i was pregnant

by him i said what is the world come to my friend shardenae was hustling up there
serving him and sh esees me

talking to him and he steps off wit her to cop and nobody said
nothing about neither
person so i fell in the trap and

now im labeled as dun dun. well they will turn around there lifes
cause stan was
drivinfg bubbles cadii and all type

of hot cars and still do and now slick was working in the goverment
and first check
was 1500 and he slipped hell do

better for u enmies who think i give a dame dont fuck wit my
babyfathers or me. andc left the block just screaming

to who ever kept bringing it up they smoke crack ok it aint my drug
of choice
miraclecc said and people can have they

own choice of drug and they still cool i just got to move on. love yah.

MY KIDS WAS AN BLESSINGS

They looked at my kids as a boon.
Like 2 doves brush woods.
Like my brassiere covered his feeding.
Repent for what you did to me.
Cleanse your soul and flesh with the Holy Spirit.
It will fill boundless.
That's my boon god.
They tried to take my chortle.

Cause they made me like Casanova cash card.
I wanted to be a bursar for my kids.
And collate in my faith.
They were so cold blooded.
I fought for my kids.
I was there cause he walked with me threw my
Hard times and sent me a mate to marry me at the end.
Mighty mother and mighty fathers.
You ran from my womb that blossomed and the
time came in th e midst and the last race was in
the next day I didn't meat that you seen the main
life in the next way I men.
Survive the way in the main voice in the year of the hand.
Surface the main tart of the mind.
You will look like the run down the pain.
Fun the name you played when you seen me
I looked like the past in the finder in the lats race.
You made me look like I was insane had me
play the game to get by im not in t eday dreams in
the person in the name I went to the snob.
you was mad I played you in the end I gave you life
you seen me you left me you said we will not
always be around the time the tables turn.

CHILD SUPPORT.....

i had just moved back to vitenam with my mom and stan didnt like
it he new i was
messing wit some one around

there so he stalked and stalked and i was the guys we meet when they were over
when mom was gon to work and.

stan had ask me was i still pregnant and i said no i just got the abortion and he told
me to come here and i said

why and went and he said something slick like thats why he told my pound of dro
and i said fuck u and ur gma

cause he was mad i was throwing bricks at his house. and he swung and we ended
up off the sidewalk in the street

and i was dogging he wit a three hit that knocked his ass out on the ground. i had
long senegalese and he pulled

them and i fell and he stoped me wit his big boots. and put a hell of a mark under my
right eye out of the four

people that was out there one stoped him from kicking me in my face and i went
back down gma house and she

called the police child support and all. so i didnt want to go to court cause my gma
called the police and we gave

them stanley LAMONT jenkins and he sid lamont wasnt his middle name in the court. so they let the case go.

and we seen he in the same white truck. he was in when we fought
that day and my
gma flag the truck. and

cursed him out about why he lyed about the situation in the court
room after she
finishtalking he walked and my

gma was beganing to call the police.

The worst thing when he died

I felt benighted.
I still hypeventited.
I was abashed and abandoned.
I need abode to rest.
A blazing my skin.
I kept ablution my skin.
He always forgave me.
The human praise an abbot like.
He was worthy.
He says praise no idol.
He knows god stood abreast of my flesh.
Till he come back to earth.
The devil not ever wins
I'll see you in heaven.
The populous in the day I seen in the funn
I was in the bank and lost to the fame I made more
cause you gave it to me you ain the placate.
Putrescent in the lover in th e name of the law in the same game
The till was empty in the race of the same main trouble in the maze.
You shame d of me look in the mirror who shame who you did.

Took the problem out on me you slick bird
with beak that run so far down the crack of the jail bars.
if you not gon to surrender in the game you will loose.
I surrender in the name of the lord in the
game of the tattoos of the hell
you will take me no more.
rabble in the midst of the day you begun in
the last maze I won the diploma
of love an a good attitude.
I pellet the name of the baddest in the n ewstar unleashed.
I seen th rai come in the nigh tan dlost t etime you
spent wit me cause you was wit the on e cause you
couldn't see the beauty I had many more gift sthen you thought
about.

When A Man Meets Temptation...

killer had just came home from jail and he new about all the foul
shit that has been
going on and miracle went in

right after he came home. it wasnt long before killer had tio meet
some fiend and
smoke with them and serve them

the dipper. and a brad came over the jail on my unit and she
explained to me cause
some how we got to talking

and she was saying killer elyise and she was bout to keep goind u
know i talk to to

much she sait she meet him bla

bla bla and i should have let her finish dumb oh me. anyway her name was tisha and
she was cool dough and she

introduce me to her connect she new i was about to be released andshe knew i
smoke the h20. and she said call

tammy she got my phone she drive shell come get u and flyy u in. and when i got
out
went threw the process and

got released as soon as i got home i called her and said whats up tammy. tisha told
me to call ur phone and u get

me and she came slam threw and we rode to the back her house her kids was i the
car and the little boy was

screamn our house is getting reventavated and i didnt know what the little boy was
saying and she was telling him

not to say nothing see tammy was an hard bargin to get threw to she was a rock and
we smoke like two dipps and i

began to scream tisha comes home. Why. cause she flew me all the in. see these was
the brads that my dude killer met when I was locked up

days went passsed me and tammy begin to hang later tisha came
home and tammy
and tish was into it about tisha

s phone bill tammy didnt pay and so we all were still friends and
when me and
tammy went to see killer. killer

served tammy and called her baby and i got mad and said dont call
ur baby she was
like he alright dont talk to

him like that and im like whole up he aint fine and dont check me
im checking mines
something had to be going

on that s why he meet them when i was locked up see i went back
and forth to
jailand so did killer and tisha. tisha

did a robbery i did a cuttery and killer did a druggery.

EMBARRASSING THINGS IN MY TEMPLE

My your body reek like old gym socks.
Cause of the bacteria I put in my flesh and my UN married sins.
It was no good it was evil.
Only for the demonstotest.
They made a bet on my life I was
Struck with my informer the lord almighty.
I was so weak for temptations.

So insular to death.
He rose on from the dead.
He made my heart beat like a jalopy.
I told you he was klaxon to your skin.
My family is like a missing follower.
Greed of the feld money hungry of the slackers.
Shield body pieces of the lost trying dunging.
The tomb of the life after your feind was lost.
In the dieing breed you preten
Is it cheating if you told me to?
You played me like abacus.
Up and downs you joked around.
Sin hear, sin there.
Use your 10 commandments if you dare.
He abandoned me and left me for dead.
He made you gamble.
He made you cheat.
He made you disrespect your parents.
He made you lay down with criminals.
He smacks you once and I let him smack you again.
God bless me for being like him.

BROKEN SOCIETY......

so u know miracle ended up pregnant she didnt know weather it
was t baby or loco
ken which was her boyfriend at

the time. u know t had took the pussy and then they began to ride
aroung and t was
booking hell of bitches fucking

all miracle friends and hood bitches and. thats how it went so how would miracle
know who baby it was if she

was sexing t in the day and loco ken at night i wouldnt be surprised if that plotted
that shit i mean all us went to

hotels and did manjajtwas. so when miracle went to the doctors that morning after
loco popped up at the window.

he was trying to wake her up sound l;ike he was the one rubbing on my feet but
even kitten woke me up like that

sometimes if it was important since my momstayed on the bottom floor. miracle was
crapping real bad after the

knock on the window. so she said alittle and said not to much and went straight to
the clinic. when loco left and

when she found out the news she was crying the whole way home and loco was on
a bike an popped up behing

miracle and said why u crying and she told him she was pregnant so i he laughed
rode off i meet huim home and

he kind of new the baby might have been t,s baby and he waiting
5 months and

landed a punch into miracle

stomache and miracle couldnt breathe and was stuck on locos bed and when she
was able to move she went to tell

her moms and daddy fiz was my moms boyfriend i guess he was coming to see if
miracle was ok. and fiz got out the

door and momma rose was holding miracle back and fiz lead loco up the stairs. And
wopped his ass loco had a

water gun in his hand cause we was playing water guns before he had hit me in the
stomach. but he got chop and

screwed inthe builded. momma rose came up wit 1400 and payed for miracle abortin
once miracle told momma

rose what happen and she didnt know who baby it was and that t had raped in her
house right before she had

walked in from work and she pouned miracle in the body. so momma rose was like
no baby here cause miracle was

only 14 years old.

WALKING AWAY

It may dissimulate you just walk away.
You have to use diverge in walking away.
Your downpour will come.
When you walk away.
You won't need a gas mask to for your pride.
I got a gash for the strong still.
It was a big gauge and a good smell.
Cause I didn't walk away
I walked away and got to make and fortress.
A living witness.
Yes I am.
Many turns the first way I know the stars of the sunshine and th elif e
Of the memories of the denin of the remedy.
Some shine so wid of the lusting ways of the player of the field why yo.
Say im like thewind in the blast of the turn ou t.
Stay low key cause im so obdurate.
Stay fly in th guest room no moor.
Obedient to the flaws.
Grandiose in th eland of the trainer in the gate of the doors.
Graceful in the stores my way or your way.
So now you flowing with the queen and you left in the libretto.
Dishearten the lost lane soften therecriut of the.
Microchip the ways of the fast.

LESSON LEARNED......

t was so forever trying to get in touch wit me for days and one day i was on the
phone at my gma house and i was

talking to my friend sandy and she said. god wrote u aletter. well he told me to write
it and read it to u. dont go out

side tonight ur enimies will attack. and i said girl u tripping and sure nuf the phone
rung on the other line. it was t

and he had this big black truck he said and i said im not coming out tonight he said im
alrady out front of ur gma

house and if u dont come out i waill start blowing and i siad go head he said he aint
playing and i said hold on

.sandy he said come outside im scared this the dude i had and abortion by. so i told
him to go beat somebody up for

me when i when i click back over and he said come on and i click back to sandy and
sandy said if u go outside

miracle i wail CALL ALL NIGHT LONG AND LET UR GMA HOLD U IN THE HOUSE.

so i said i was gone leave it off the hook and i did. and went outside it wa an all black
truck and two niggas in the

back and ha don ski mask and i said im not getting in until they take off there ski
mask and one of them replyed

and i said rico and he took the mask off i think i blew his cover. and then the other
probably said well let me take

off mines and it sure was rico the first one and dame me and rico use to smoke
heavy when i had crack the big safe

open and had hella weed every morning before we went to high school. man any
way i got in after rico shook up

the pcp and t aint a had
to say no more bam and then we scruted 0ff and went to the hill by the grave and
smoke hell of dipps and then t

said he was taking the home rico and his man whoever he was. and when we got to
the otherside of ne from uptown

smoking and rico and his man got out the car and rico had on a big as winter coat in
the summer time im

wondering why and when rico and his man came back out the house they came to
side of the car and t was talkin

to some lady and whoever truck it was and never got off the phone and rico had
pulled out a shoot gun telling me

he sending me to heaven wit kitten and soulface and i was like man what we knew
each other this ling why u going

on me like that. and t sitting there on the phone like he dont see whats going on and
the gun on his side iseen the gun

when he walked up and it was hanging from his coat and i been told t to pull off and
and he sat there thats what

he called me out the house for he was mad cause i ghad an abortion and rico was
mad kept screaming about some

money i stole. man i seen was the gun and five bitches come from outone side of
the alley and another five come

from other side of the alley and i got to punching t in the face pull off and the brad
scream 5-0. and i was like

dame. and t pulled three blocks to the old car lot and i hopped op and stabbed al

80

l the tires on the bitch truck

whoever it was so he wouldnt be able to get me. so i flew in the middle of the street
he jumps out pulls his pistol from

under my sit and faces it at me as im running in the middle of the street. and i said if
i died tonight in the street

somebody will see me hit the ground and i ran to the car lot across the street and hid
for like 5 hours. i tryed to

hoped the brick wall coulnt get over it cause i heard a car on the leaves come toward
me i just new it was ty it

happen to fast and his tires aint go all the way down yet they tryed to murk me and i
wasnt havent it. so when the

the car left i almost pissed on my self trying to hide and i left the hiding spot bout
dawn and some niggas was outside

so i called the cops and they ask me was i high and i said yeh but im good and they
tryed to kill me and too me to

the station and called my peoples to come get me cause they thought i was
launching. shouldnt have listen to sandy.

at the polic eprecent tripping. anyway time goes pass and rico ended up shooting
hisself in the
foot and had a cast on and t had did some time t was so trying to kill me while kitten
was alive he pulled a nine on

me cause i had abortion he crazy.

TEMPTATION

Temptation will be like and wild beast coming to you.
A Terries in heart.
Torture to our blood.
A hideous burn.
You better convert us to the lord.
You will have no respect.
Your body will be rotten.
This is the conflict.
There will be no justification.
You will have no scarification to be made holy in the end.
This theory.
Driven by the panic of the voices of the creame of the latest.
Handle all the pain in the scence of the kindom of the
waisted one in the season.
Yeh we sung the town in the night th e.
Time has come the latest person in the sunrisen
in the first step in the last round in the forplay
it s all good in the back ground you played me so I could hear you.
you played with the right one in the nexst life. Youll see the famine.

mine and yours is the first ways to see you in the pasat in the last
run down.
well im in the last mission.

vitenam
when kevin was banging he had it all and he had family that was in
my building on
the second floolr and he was

making so much money he ha dfronting me and kitten some coke
and we sold it.
one day i had went out with the

family my mom and fiz and when we had got back. we had seen the
street blocked
off and we couldnt park on the

street cause the feds was in the street and we had to go through the
alley and park
and walk around. so when we

got to the steps of the apartment. we seen a coat laying in the middle
of the street
and everybody was saying that

like what happen while my mom went up the steps wit fiz and they
said kevin was
serving some niggas miracle and

the niggas in the back had open the door on the right and gave him
a fake 20 dollar
bill and kevinsaid give him

his dum bag back and the nigga was from over leon terrace u know leon terrance
was beefing with vitenam for a

long time this is years of beefing. so the nigga pulleg out the gun and began to bust at
kevin and try to close him in

the door and drag him down the street and he reached for his gun to bust back in
the car and he didnt survive and

the nigga toolie was out there wit his mack and he got in the middle of the street and
let it loose and hit a nigga in

the back the car swerverd and the y got loose. and i got so high that night i smoke on
the roof and had a
net long hoodie on that came to my knee. and was so high i was walking outside wit
that on alway to the store went

loco ken and his siter and friends even after we fought. rip kevin. u dies like g.

Do Want A Color Change

I am marvel inside and out.
Sometimes a minimizing heart is good.
Let's build a great fellowship for him.

You need guidance to light.
He will redeem you.
It is so unbelievable.
Don't be cruel to my skin.
Let's not have despair of him.
Believe in him in the deed.
He'll be there to save you.
He comes in time.
He mounted in heaven.
As you approached him you will have to believe to be a Christian.
Your will your life you choose your path.
If you choose the pit you will get a color change.

time for hair and lust.......
well miracle been started hair school in 08 and miracle kapt getting
locked up or

pregnant. thats why she coludnt

get her ged. she was transfer over to the other beauty school in nw
cause she was
living in the goonies and she was

pregnant so she went to the school until she became to far in the
pregnancy. and
she had to relax and lay up cause

some how she alays had preeclampsia with her pregnancy. so after
she had the
baby london she went back cause u

know tez and manman had been taking frome her by her gma cause
she was
launching and really writing a book

and they were maybe not wanting miracle to be successful cause
they were scared
the same thing that had happen

to her father was going to happen to her. u know how daddy shane
died over the
jail. well any way the day miracle

came back u know the niggas be rolling in the hair salon when they
getting a free hair
do. so it was one guy

miracle had her eye on and its always the red one and she always
ends up with the
loveable hard core black niggas
so miracle was doingth ered guy hair and conversating. with him
then a guy had
came and sat in the next booth

and my friend was doing his hair and me and him begin to argue
about wha race can
do hair better black people

or african and i said everybody is good and he said they braid better
and i said no
cause he was getting cornrows

and i know alot of black woman know how to bang some corn rows.
so as the time
went on we seen each other

again and again miracle was coming in the school for an program
speech and was
entering the bathroom and it

was unisex and he was in there. when miracle openthe door and he
was comeing
out she asked him was he going to

the program and he said yeh and he waited for miracle to come out
the bathroom
and said his name was unique.

and we enter like an stylish couple. and we sat down right next to
each other. And
he asked if i had a jack and i

said naw i ended up buying two from thwe girl next to be name
bonnie and who
would have knew. so he sai dhe

wanted to go smoke them and we left went out front and we talked
and then he
said he was leaving so i said i might

as well go to. so he said u need a ride and i said yeh and u gone take
me to my
daughter and he said yeh and we

went to my deturbing gma house the one that always says go home
miracle like a
nucience. so i picked her up cause

london sits there while i go to school at night. so we went the store
and went
straight to drop me off home unique ask

me to get his hair done and i said yeh come on up and we talked
and he said can i tell

u something u r just my type

and ur im very attracted to u and i was like oh. so the night went
by he left and he
came back wit a roach and was

smoking it and he said man what u gon do so i look ed at him i was
in heat i went to
ease my way to get a condom

and he said whats this and i said u dont know. and he must didnt
want to use a
condom and so he bent this ass over

and dogged the pussy made it so wet that. we could have made a
baby and i told
him that if i was to get pregnant

i was going straight tot he abortion clinic cause i was in love with
some one and we
was getting married. so it came

around again when he called and i was supened for throwing big
gel can at a bitch
and tap her jaw for being slick

oyt the mouth i had niggas dropping of my work fromth eteacher
miss lopez. so he
came over and laid in my bed

and had on some orange jaiol boxer we fucked that what i call a
nigga like that and
he actullay laid in my bed

and said he had a girl after round to some days later and i said what
he wouldn't
repeat his self i just want ed to

make it clear i told that nigga ill call u wheni found out if im
pregnant so 6 weeks later
i cvalled the doctor and she

said i was 2 week slate and to come i the office. and after i got my
paper work
saying i was six weeks pregnant and i call number.
that's was a anothother story.

I CHANGE FOR MY KIDS

I was innocent still in cruel still in cruel hideous places.
I was like an exhibit to the earth.
I converted myself to go to heaven.
Recognize my glow and glory.
You will be rotten if you don't change.
I told myself I like Epicureanism.
So I stoicism myself at church.
I broader my heart.
You are a heathen is it ok to come to god?
He will embrace you.
You have to listen to the principles and you will live long.
Strive for your kids, he did for us.
You have many no bless to learn.
It's not intricate to follow.
You have doctrines to follow.
Fight for Christianity

Man oh man I iknow I sse the goals of the
past of the last life of the.
fortitfication

death before the alter....

it was a tragic day they meet kitten and soulface. he was the type if
he coulnt have
u nobody can so he percificly

said that kitten could only talk to miracle and star and thats was it
he was so
demanding a little demand is good in

a man not a whole lot doe. so we had met me and kitten cause i was
outside with my
faggy friend joel and we was

about to get a dutch and and we ask could kitten go and he said yeh
cause i was
already dating the nigga from

vitenam name loco ken we was already together for a while see me
and kitten
connect off jump she said whats up

bitch and was so little i was so fired up the next day i seen her i said
whats up winch
so after he allowed her to go to

the store we went to the back of the school yard to smoke were no
one finished and
was to young to be in highschool

anyways. so we smoke cause the enviroment taught us and the streets raised us
. kitten and i had a long

conveseration and she told me she was on the run as a juve for running inthis brads
house im like little shorty go

hard. so we smoke like three j and as i start to hang with kitten more i wander away
from loren and we in up

separeted as friends loren had it bad her mother was hard on her so she had to fend
for her self and she did just that

as a teen. she just needed positive guidance and i was headed for failure at the time
so i wasnt a good friend at the

time and she was trying to make. so back to kitten we walked back to soul face and
he made her go in thwe house

everyday something was going on broken doors whole sin the wall soulface was
crazy and he didnt take his meds he

just held his gun. so he was so obcessed wit kitten if kitten left his site he couldn
t cell his drugs good. dont get me

wrong he supported his kitten. so it kinda felt like kitten was an agel she always came around when i needed

love and attenion
I flew over to the other side of ne and he was there and he was off
his launching shit
to an dhe was sitting on the

washing machine that was outside under th porch saying he was
lucifer and the
devil, and satan i began to leave

kitten was like hold up i need to talk to jhim and he said nothing
he just began to get
his ass wooped cause kitten got

to swinging at this 6 foot tall man and and he had dragged her out
through the
bottom part of the door and said

miracle tell her stop so i began to walk and say im calling her mother
and he was
after me wit the gun so after

kitten wrapped her hair and she came out front cause it happen out
back the fight
and al she said was come on lets

get some jack s and he left and the next week she was gone killed in
the basement
and that was his at house im

surprised his aunt didnt here the gun shot and he killed his self that
s amean joint
love u kitten.

HE UNFORGETTABLE TO ME

Hess the philosophy of heaven.
This humanity is for fools.
The universdeath before the alter
all power of freedom.
He gives you morality and a new one.
He so tremendous to my soul.
You have many virtues to change.
Surrender your life for someone he did.
Hess like good opium.
That's my doctrines to survive.
He embraces me all day and night.
If you live moral he will take your life.
I'm the foundation he sent until he comes.
The word to pass on.
My forgiveness to him.
I love my god.
Do you.
Ask and you shall receive.
He will lay and hand on you r heart.
If you don't answer he will have you suffer.
If you don't vagunce he won't hear you.
Learn to show the hardest in the mal frame.
You shine so hard in the fountain of the seed glowing like the
miseltoe.
And the rain that shined in the paths of the funning setting.
This is the game plan of the season.
Likeable of the rin down down drama queen and the planner.
You can say the same thing in the fortune in the planner.
And how you seen the gift of the people

time for hair and lust part2
he said whats up miracle and i said im pregnant what u gon do u gone give me the
money. so he said pause and ill

see what i can do and he said ill call u back. so we texted and i siad come threw and
he said when i said now and he

said not now and i said when u comig then and i got no reply so i called the back and
it was and girl and i said

can i speak to unique. she said you got the wrong number and i said no he just call
me and she said oh u talking

about jermaine and she put her mom on the phone and she said who is this i said his
baby mother and she said im

his girl and we argued and i wa like u must not able to have kids wit him cause why
he over here and we went on

and on. and then ring ring after me and the so called girlfriend hung up. it was the
jermaine guy i havet met yet
i met unique. and he said what u say cause he must couldnt go in the house. so he
came after 3 weeks and only

brought half the dough and i didnt have my half so he had to come again i mean he spent the night and tryed to

run my crib. so i went back to school after the subspenision was over
and there he
was and getting his hair did u

know i had ask the teacher did she know he before subspenision and
she said no
and then yeh wheni found out his

real name and he took one of her classes. so come to find out after
we finish the

heads for the day it was going on

about 9 pm at night. me and the brad bonnie walked to the store
and she said she
was going to buy me a pack of

newtys and the jacks and i said yeh so bout time we exit the school
she brought
unique up and i was liuke the dumb

bitch dont even know his name. i was like he told me the same thing
in my head.
and she began to talk and i said

wel how u know all this about him she said he gave her a ride i said
all he trying fuck u
he did the same thing to me

dont ever tell a female who u smash on ur mans. so i wanted to
smack the dogg shit
out of her but i was like naw

let me get these jacks. and the next time at school see i had told the teacher
everuything i started to think she wanted

him cause they start getting tight and then she kept putting bonnie on his hair i mean
wghen i started thta school

bonnie was the first person i talked to her and the other girl see bonnie was a dog
walker so she can have his ass and

i taled her i broght her agift my left overs. the teacher new she was starting a mess u
new my temper so bonnie left

fromdoing unquie hairs just to come bother me and throw it in my face and say hi
miracle i said girl u better get

out my face she begin to laugh so i said girl ill beat the shit out of u and she laughed i
said step outside and the

teacher come miracle u got to go. and we ran in to security and they siad whats
going on and we explained they

messing with me she fucking a nigga i was pregnant by she didnt even let me get the
baby out before she jumped on

deck. bitch so i left got my diploma and not ever cameback until 5 months when i needed my ends clip and he was

there and she wasnt i told her he aint gon get u pregnant if her
wanted u he would
have got u first and u know he

only trying to get my attention but hoes be geeking for ur dick see
he didnt even tell
me about his girl till i was

already prego say beet it bitches.

THE WAY TO LEARN

Pray for salvation.
He all hears you.
Believe in your heart.
Bow down now.
Before you walk the steps he calls you.
If you repent he will chastise you and leave you.
If you repent he will restore you.
This is my testimony to you.
You have more ethics to learn.
Open a book.
Go to a quiet place.
Praise him.
He's divine.
He won't change on you.
The devil will learn.
In the end.
We all will be god's children.

Unstoppable.
Stomp the devils hand in sinners.

waiting for love.....
so i kept sending killer money on the phone and he was calling home speakingto the
baby and me and we was

planning our wedding. he missed the birth the preganacy and the baby birthday and
i took pics. so he kept saying

every month he was coming home and i still seen no killer and i called the warden
and he said he will see what he

can do to get him in the halway house since he was eligible and in about 3 week s i
had got a call im in the halway

house this killer and i was so happy and he came home. and beat the pussy up. he
alwayed prayed we got married

even off the love boat. and bout a month we went to the cort build ing and filled out
the papers. so we had to wait

another 3 weeks. i felt a little nervous about is it going to work or is he really the
one we already had been together

for 7 1/2 years and had a baby and he claimed all the kids and i was just so happy and when the weeks was over it

came may 15 2013 we met up down the court building. i thught he was standing me
up cause i couldnt find him

and he showed and we went to the 4 th floor and signed in and i was so glad that he
loved me threw my health
issues and all thick and thin. it was like we belonged and now were joined together
with god and the we made love

like babck to back and it was a blessing to finaaly not be sinning making love.

WHO UNDERSTANDS ME?

Cherish me he said.
Make me whole.
You will live abundant he said to you.
I found myself wedged in the jail.
He said hey yonder my child.
I predicted you were mine long time ago.
I litter you here from heaven.
I gave you breathe and birth you to human form
He said I brought you my massive burdens.
If you're desolated call me.
It's unexplainable how you will live after death.
The devil will tidal you from me.
I'm the only one to unleash those chains.

It's a mystery how he talks to me.
He so luscious.
He my husband.
My shield, my protector.
My inhabitants live in the earth and soon heaven.
I will let him make you ripe.
If you bloc your our ears.
I'm calling.
Let me in.

dairy page..187...
killer began to change his life when he was released he was going to the church
being a good father and and mate.

we havent even fought yet and im surprised cause he used to drag me throught he

alleys and pour beer on my name

my mothers age getting married and she missed her chance to get married momma
rose was asked to get married

whe n she was around my age and she passed it up so i just inded wasnt going pass it
. u know im in to my rapping

thing an di just hope that as me marring this guy killer that he wont. abbuse use an
dphycally emontinally hurt

me and u know 2 niggas was trying to marry me at the same time mitchel and killer and of i picked killer and

mitch was a good dude he gave me the world and every paycheck
300, 600 durning
tax time but he lived with his

baby moms and i couldnt do that see i was already preganant by
him to and then the
girl called and i was trying

to get some boat forme and killer see killer father was a pimp he
kinda had in him to.
i think i did make the best

choice. i mean mitch is like way obbessed and if someone says hi he
gets mad that's
how i am over killer and thats

how killer baby moms is over him and it was just a cycle i mean the
reason why i
really didntg want to marry

mitch he tryed to cut me cause its was a guy coming over to get
some k2 and we
suppose to ben going to the

reaturant and mitch was mad and jealous i couldnt go threw that
io killer is a lyer and
not an protector and

mitch is i dont know what i did. ps god made the decision he
already new.

HOW TO FIND HIM

You already found me.
When you touched this book.
You just displaced ourselves in the lords hands.
New life just became on you.
There clusters of the devil everywhere.
Watch out for him.
Blind you and you.
Suffer badly.
I would make you suffer to.
It's a good suffer.
Like it's hard to get money.
The devil predicted that for you.
He would recede you.
There's only one life.
Live right for me.
To you, to me, I love you.
If your love one didn't tell you today.
Your enemies may tell you before them to deceit your mind its trickery.

gotta get......
well i started to hang with porcha and porcha would smoke and and drink beer and
she had an milfunction and

when she did that. so it would happen right in front of the nigga sshe would shit and
piss on her self and i would be

like dame u would never know cause she would end up stepping off she aint give a
fuck just like i didnt give a fuck

about my sweating disorder i m talking about bad bitches with disorder. man
whitney and tish wa tricks they act

like they wasnt but see i wouuldnt call it an trick cuse we all could get money with no
problem. its either we wanted

to sex u or not if we just plain ohll wanted wanting ur money or ur drug best believe
we would get and it wouldnt be

a problem.

DO YOU NEED FAST MONEY?

I know a remedy for your stinky fingers.
It's a destination a will.
You ask and you will give you must be specific.
I'm not just giving to a cruel heart.
I know if your heart is change.
Believe me.
I feel your pain.
I sit right beside you.
I breathe when you breathe.
I sense what you sense
I'm your usher.

They holy spirit will lead you to me.
I will appoint you to guide others.
This is judgment heaven and earth.
Why you think you got to go to jail.
Cause you sin.
That's your punishment.
The devil sends you there.
Because you appointed you listen to his wicked ways.
Suddenly.

robbery.... miracle and tish was riding in her jeep and they picked
up. porcha see
porcha and tish new each other
since the sand box they would say so we pulled up to my house and
we was looking
for the water and seen the key to

the crip and was in the door and tish was like go in see tish was
really red with green
eyes and had an hee; of

attitude she already had an robbery charge for robbing the gallery
and now this
when i turn the key and went in

iwalked aroungd and the drug man and his girl was slepp and then.
i looked around
for the stash i found coke and

h20. so i took the h20 and dipped we ran through the alley and hit
the car told
everybody to get out threw the keys

and went t o get high see renold was whitney friend he shouldnt have been with us
anyway and. and he smoke and

cuff the shiyt everybody new he had it and then he went home and call for a ride to
get high i mean. he was a mess

. me and tish was like we put in the work and an dme and tish got in to it when we
was dropping renold home and

he had to brake it up beacuse tish tryed to swing cause i kept blaming her and i
swung her and she walked off her

ad porcha. tryed to apolgize but she wasnt just gon hit me neighter so oh well i let
her bee mad for a minute cause

we all would take turns treating ecah other out me tisha an whitney so our friends
ship meant alot to me.

THIS IS MY LASTING IMPRESSION

I didn't forsake you.
I not ever left you.
Even if you did me wrong.
You accepted me.
I persuading your minds.

I'm that powerful.
You sinners.
I love you.
I will change you eternity.
Hold on.
It will get better.
I feel your brain is like I can't finish.
You hold on.
Take the humiliation.
That's the goal.
It seems hard.
It's not.
The devil makes you think it's hard.
Strive for the sweetness.
For I make you sink in the bitter disgust.
My threshold is where I sit.
No one can take my place.
You have to be determining to sit next to me.
You try to beat my power.
I will send you flying to hell.
Difference between freedom and bars
Conviction is for the demonic spirits I capture.
That's why I told you I held the devil in chains for years.
That's what I conceived and he turned against me.
I love my enemies.
Which means I also love him to.
If He repents he shall change to.
Make your decisions right.
This is your recovery.
Adam and eve
Thank you for your good and bad ways
The taught me.
You're like Adam and eve.
I bit the wrong tree.

You thought I was rotten.
Well I was I became a rose.
Out of the rotten tree.
I bit the wrong tree.
I bit the wrong lover.
And he gave me the depths of hell.
So I turned away sooner than you think.
They not ever told me to please.
First obey the 10 commandments.
You will be blessed.
Listen to his will bow down all your wrongs will disappear.
Lift your hands to the king you will have rest.

kitten soul was released.....
the night kitten was killed i was over woody house she wanted to
go see luckster
and get ten and i was like lets walked

together and she was like ill meet u and i was like we never seperate
why do u want
to seprate now and she was

suppose to go spend a night at my house and i went back down
wood house and
never seen for the whole week when

we left each other it was saturday and and i looked up th eone way
and didnt see
her after i got my ten to get the

h20. so then i went down lessie house and she said that her and jim
went home
and i didnt feel like going al the

way over there and that sunday night i felt kitten get killed she was pregnent with a
gun shot womb to the head

and to the stomach and i was hearing the gun shot wombs in my sleep and seeing
her walk up vitnenam and
i was calling her and she wouldnt respond or look back and i came up town that
tuesday morning cause i thought

she was gon come back around and i didnt see her so i went home back uptown. so
when i arrived my gma said

someone keeps calling and i said who the phone ring about 20 minutes later and it
was angel from vitenam i was

trying to firgue out how she got my number i firgue she found it or got it from her
dude,and she said miracle kitten

got killed jim killed her and i said no. so i called kittens mother,pat and i ask her is
muffin ok and she replyed with

ONLY GOD CAN JUDGE ME

I fill missing
Cause I lost my best friend.

She went chasing the wind.
Which she thought it was clean.
But it was polluted.
She was hurt in many ways.
Physically, sexually and mentally.
She smiled to hide the hurt.
She lived with the sorrow and pain.
She cried constantly.
She ran from the blues.
She hid be hide the bars of the streets.
She functions with sanity.
Which I mean was it necessary
It was only for the things.
That growled on the trees.
Her beauty was unconditional.
I felt the gunshots in my sleep.
All I seen was her smile and her walking the one way on 21 sites by the gas station.
All I hear is her voice crying lying in the ground birthing.
Why must we suffer?
I will meet u again.
My Unborn child
My lucisious unborn child.
I felt the strength of his veins.
He's like a rose sprinkling inside.
How much beauty.
I fell of my unborn child.
Oh how I love to hear my unborn child voice.
His eyes, his lips, his skin.
The softness of his tender skin.
Of his first sight a memory that I will not forget the sun shine that shines and gives a light to my inside.
Oh the brown skin Chocó complexion.
My lucisious unborn child.

A solid heart
I have a solid heart.
Well, that's what everyone else thinks.
But my heart is soft as cotton.
It blows with the wind.
Only if I could grab my heart and rip it apart.
I will el no more pain.
I have a solid heart.
Well that's what everyone else thinks.
But my heart is as weak as a cloud.
Sometimes I think I have a whole in my heart.
Because it hurt so roughly.
Just this one spot hurts.
Like someone makes my heart hurt.
I have a solid heart.
Well that's what everyone else thinks.
Like someone makes my heart bleed of pain.
I have a solid heart.
Well that what everyone else thinks.
I cry with a passion to.
I cry when I'm happy to.
I cry because I'm so sad to.
I have a solid heart.
Well that's what everyone else thinks.
How I got here
All I here is gunshots of no spacious color.
Going through my brain.
Am I going insane?
Luckily I got my glock on my waist.
Attach to my case.
I got off from my case.
To go to another race.
Pentacle penalty and I'm not ashamed of the chains.
I got a baby on the way.

Still I survive the birthing pains.
A black panther.
Who not ever died?
Gunshots come clearly.
Once I get you.
They come clearly with no name.
It's branded for life.
It's suffering womb.
Father can you help me through the pain.
The streets gates won't close for me.
Now how far am I away from the gate of yours?
I didn't get no for an answer.
I have to pocket a womb.
I thought I ran from the fire.
But the heat is so close to me.
Keep seeing this man in black attacking me.
Shackles and cuffs.
Hurting my wombs.
While my family watches me from their seat
And my lover screaming I want my money back for bail.
Praying that this jail will let me succeed.
6 more months till labor.
I fill worse and worse.
Take my burden lord.
Can I hear the gunshots?
Streets bloody the Mary.
God take me.
Why must I go through the things of daily life?
Why must I feel? Hurt.
Why she said or he said.
Why would you give my feelings away?
God take me away.
You took my other half.
Why not me.

God stop saving me
Help me to bleed to cry to die.
Why, I think I bleed so long and cried monthly.
So it's time for me to die you said.
I'm tired of feeling these feelings of no man world.
God take me from the sin.

too high.
see i had meet this dude name selim and he was a money getting
nigga he was one
of my tricks. it was a one time

thing and were i wanted to get me and my dude high killer. so killer
act like he didn't
know what i was doing but

he didnt care. so i did and we had no money. so this nigga started
to give me the
world. we was ride in the jeep and

he didnt know i was pregnant by killer cause i had had an abortion
by him cause it
wasnt meant i mean i didnt

mean to get pregnant and he was a good man just wasnt my type.
he was to
obbessed and overly aggressive so we

seen his man lupas and he had a girl wit him we was at the gas statio
getting gas and
he had broke down and so

happen. they said they wanted to be dropped off and get something
really quick

from up the street and we drove an

ended up in the projects on the boat strip. so the guy never came so they ask me
and i told them i cheif and they said

were its at. so i brought them to the boat strip over london place. they got two i
brought one.
and then me and selim drop them off and we went to selim brother house and they
were smoking tree and i just had

two h20,s. so they smoke like 6 js and i left and selim followed. if i would had
stayed ant longer i would have

earled on the couch. bout time i got to the truck and selim got in and i got in i had to
get right back out, cause ifelt

my mouth watering and went i got ou ti spit up like and gushing fire extingusher and
fell out and couldnt get up

and was ouit for about 5 minutes going into a cesure and broke my leg and swelim
looked and walked around the

car after it happen he talked about it looked like the exdousis,. i scared him and i
could have miscarriage and

everything and i should have called the ambulance but i tryed to drive on my hurting
leg well it was sprained not

and it hurts. and he was trying to get so pussy while i was in pain and we argued i
called the police cause he gotta

broke. so when we had got back to my crib selim said miracle can i lay wit u. i said no
cause i got to stretch my leg

asking for the clothes he brought me some days ago how inconsiderated that u
would try to get some pussy while i

was in pain. so the next morning i called the ambulance and yep it was sprained.

TESTED

I sit back and sit in the days were living in.
Is all attest of my comprehension of lust of these worldly things?
I will graduate in the will of the lord.
Well you saw me falling deeper and deeper.
Throw the rope I pulled myself back up.
But hey you told me I wasn't ready to come
Back to the light so I pretended to be a slave.
I still fill a little down and I was tested of the grave.
So I can blow my brains back of the opium.
Leave me alone I'm screaming for the help.

The proportion of the eyeballs out of the socket seeing the invisible.

Body bleeds inside of the tested tec.

Another charge he told you fools.

Take loose of my pants why life has to be so made of fishy sex.

Tested to the cheaters.

What's right and what's wrong

They constantly attack me.

They think I will respect the negative wrongs of this life.

What's right is right what's wrong is wrong.

I'll only loose if I fight the weather of this world alone.

This town is weird.

They want me to be what they want me to be.

What right is right what's wrong is wrong.

They took me for the hostage.

To demonstrate my mind.

Maybe I'm blind of myself.

What right is right what's wrong is wrong.

Want what you can't have

Sex me, sex me, and sex me.

Insert me down.

Paint that what the devil told you to do.

How you want to carry me.

Step in my circle lets go to my world.

7 shoots to Ur head if you fail to take my fever.

Well I watch your blood escape from your head.

I see your picture on that t shirt.

You will not ever die in my mind.

Oops isn't that and surprise.

First you didn't know me.

You saw my eyes.

Before you seen the judge.

First you were upset because you couldn't understand me.

Looking in my eyes and seeing pain.

Because you took my world when you took me off the steps.

7 times you caught me.
Sex me to I was demolished till no one would want my love
Wanted it
I felt shutdown.
Mixed up in the game.
Everybody against me.
They don't know what they're up against.
So I feel ashamed not at all.
Wasted my goodies on the street.
You took my body not my soul.
You can have my flesh not my soul it's already token by god.
The way I'm gone break you done is wit this writers pad.
You wanted for a long time.
So I'm gone give you this ink not my body.
What you need for the survival of the fullest.
2 black eyes and maybe a fracture skull.
You broke my bones and took my son for granted and married to the family.
You were acting like you wanted it for a long time.
You take my kindness for a weakness.
It been like this for a long time no love for me the streets don't even love me.
Thinking you gone test me.
T. for the terminator.
Cause you took my family and split the rose and dipped it to the wrong tree.
I would explain the rest because you wanted it for a long time.
M. stands for mislead into this marriage how you got
To this door step you couldn't get me so you got to my line.
You doing it to Ur self.
C for the confidence that you got to lay down to join in
I already know you looking for gold and an easy way for the life.
You were acting like you wanted for a long time.
Amusement to the abusement

Smokey lighter
Smokey sit tight
Hold on right
Bubbling champion
Turning to rain
Smokey lighter
Smokey sit tight
Cozy as he sat
With arms around my neck
Laughing at the whole picture.
Smokey lighter
Smokey sit tight.
Hold on right
Ripped out of the sock it
Bones of the rearranges like bozo the clown you had me feel.
Frown I made of you
Breakable tire glass
It hurts like hot tea.
Hearts of a million men laughing at me.
Hold on right.
While ill mix you with algebra.
Forget your radius.
I am the circumference.
Rebirth me.
Long leash held you down.
Dismiss this sheep.
Face like a dice.
I couldn't cut you and you got it anyway.
This collar was real tight for my son.
Hold on right you couldn't pay me enough to smile for that night.
Forgive not forgotten.
Smokey lighter.
Blood against water.
Thought we was a thicker than that.

Barred from my own wake.
Scratching your mind
Made men you say.
Quick to point the finger.
No remorse he told you to do it.
Busted in the heart pounding like mars to Jupiter.
Hold on right
Smokey lighter.
Renaissance
Dogs are characters
Nasty as they are
They piss and squat.
Long as a rabbit tooth
Plastic covers leopard prints.
Poke a dot skirt
Red stripes on my jeans hollow night massacre sheets
Bosom of the lecture
Tales of the hoodoo leave me alone witch craft
My emotional sin
Why plead guilty dogs of the war you called me invisible.
You called me to play with the dogs.
You went plundering
Playtime is over
Ash to grass
Birds of the wheel
Black hawks
Looking for attention
You knew I was hurt
Snake to snake
Cowards of the must
Should I penetrate?
My eyes on the prize
Love me dearly you thought
From that speck in your eye

I knew you disliked my walk
Doing me in the light
I sang a trumpet to see my daddy again
Burning fire you taught me wrong
Destiny arrives
Dust my feet at your door
Dies from the rules
This is a game of spades
Saved by the bell
He shot you
Reminisce in me

WORDS OF THE STEEL

Last of the words
You notice I sunk in the red ink
Chained to my room door and sent away
So you could love the adopted
You raped me and the orphan
Book and found me threw a child
This is train smoke climbing my balcony
You enter the lasts days
I did my time my 30 days was up
Lonely little prophet I sat
Angel comes to rescue me from this lonely world
They don't love me they love my money
Separated like a game of chess
Lonely problems bring on this battle
Tell me another lye
sins will sank you so long and lasting
preparation for a casket

Play your part and I will play my knight
Horse men trapped in the left lane
I blame no one for my lost one
No cheese on this trap and I still caught you
The cat got your weapon
The alley bats ride through thirteen ways
You even shook seven street walls.
Doomed to the foot prints of love
Help did you call on me did I hear you say a name
You think you slipping now
You showed me no remorse threw the town
You spoke on my troubles
Like this was gone last
Unconditional raped is that how we bound
Running in my house letting the orphan smoke your tree
I knew you was a snake and now you sank
Pay back I did not
I left it all in the hands of the god
640 in the morning
Sending your dollars at me I hope you got paid for my donkey
While my body was interesting to you
Wrapped to the toilet
Sparkling clean your liver was shedding skit in my belly
Early I seen you cousin to cousin
I'm gone miss this you and slave can have the game I'm gone
I told you I was gone take the plane trip
You charge me and it still isn't stop my shine

fire extigintisher...
man oh man i got that extishiuer. it twas the fight night of weather
or not tish and
whitney was sleeping with
with killer and whinety kept calling miracle stupiud and then tish
was stand in

antonishing look. and kept

agonizing miracle ur a stipud bitch ur an stupid bitch. and
constantanly miralcle was
followng tish and whitney

down the street. cause of the aroused comments and they were
leaving her. so
miracle ran down to the corner of the

block and screamed on whitnety tish said nothing and they just
lolilgag down the
street for there pricless friendship

to exclude miracle out the bunch cause if miracle didnt have any
well beings for
them they didnt care or they did

and they started to think we dont need her car we can get around
by foot see the
group took turns gatherinfg evrey

boby out to eat. and so then. so miracle ran back home to get the
grabbed the fire
extisher and drove down th e

street to let whitney know what was goo and drove around the whole
east captiol
and was like. who stupid who

stupid now bitch and sprayed her with the fire extishuer. and she
had looked like
frosted the snow woman. so now

whitney was chasing miracle car around in circle she wasnt faster
then the car but
for her to have some type of

boldness i liked it cause she was chasing a car looking like frosty ice
man. so any way i
pulled.off. thats when we had

a bad vibe with each other. so as times and days passe whitney gma
ended up
dieing and she was the sweetest had

the longest hair and she was going threw it so i just left it alone unitl
tish called me
. and i asked her what happen

to whitney and was she ok.

TAMPERED WITH A 2 $ TRICK

11 gage trick bag
Treat this trick
Don't trick me
I'm hip on the brick
Prostitute you love for the high
A million $ baby DRAWN TO THE STRRET FOR LESS love
Mile stone is the way she ran free
Free from paying for a man high brain you
Lesser than an woman trick house kids
Feed by the brain of a slut you called your self
Country boys off the set

Together we ran the haunted tables
They scatter like jersey guys
Against the will I slept with your senders
Taste the chest of my blood
It was like the music of the color code
The cult of the breed of your cousin seed calling you daddy
Choose the hundred twice you paid for her boots
You brought me a line of leftover shoes
This culture was lost
A sense of confusion trying to get me to sex your uncle
Anxiety fails you arrest me for the lost soul I would not compare to
So you saluted the block hard to find the trick next door
I read your closet you queen
Hide yourself you had the nerve tell me in jail threw the word.
Shy I will not
Not barn or the stalk you thought I was
It just it's complete
No answer is more motivated to me
Than the lies you told on me
Who stole your weapon your right hand man standing in your face?
Laughing sealing your tree
This vine is not for you any more
You drain my sex juices
With bacteria for days
No you got your cousin seed
He screamed for the outlet
I sat confused. You made my seed sex me. Cause you seeded with
yours
It wasn't my will I told u to show the truth
Threw the experience of the love one and an friend
I told you my rape and you let it go threw
One ear and out the other and go me locked up for
Telling you the truth end the end he took you hostage
You held me in a room with a skeleton key and tried to g me

You knew you ran and disappeared
And told me I wanted it like this for a longtime
If you was mislabeled I would be to
I still loved my rapers and blessed them
No way out so I played my cards
Mother paid to know my trick
You drove that car and lost your life

3 IN 1

3 hawks in a pit
1 left to watch
2 snakes and 1 around my neck
Help me angel
Guardian angel
Your princess was robbed and defiled of life
Little camel
Little Japanese
Come back to me
Like a hawk made on the barrels
Ride spree wheelers
Dust the camels
Hump to hump we ride
Comeback to me
Ride spree wheelers
Dust to dawn
Flying like camouflage smoke
Invisible faces
Mask of the donkey
Sprinkle my chest.

Looks like snow
Falls like snow
Menstrual flows from my eyes.
Sheds tears of hate
Hump to hump.
Little Japanese
Come back to me
Like a hawk made on the barrels
Ride spree wheelers
Looks like snow
Falls like rain
Out the camel butt
Sheds tears of the hate hump to
Hump dislikes little spirit Japanese.

2 HAND

Shadow threads along the willow path
Through the dust of the despairs
Creepy cries
Walks and taunts
Weakness
Hurts me flatters my cry
Lonely footsteps
As I survive
Hiding in the dust
Left in the pain
Rapped in the cotton
Back like fist
Holding me like fear
Green pastures

Lily chirps
Rolling stones
Happy psalms
Whisper willows
Hidden jewels
Lonely good byes
Chariot slide
Sweet cries
Cherry burst
Yellow bricks
Skittle curses
Long roads
Suddenly found
Birds of the gem
Taunts of the crime
To be or not to be
Marriage dies
Got you
Super intelligence
Yet you're so talkative
Blooper sin city
Writing notes
Concubine
Lolipoppers.
Super talkative.
Very intelligent
Boxer not to be
Finish my daddy's job
Got you

CHAPTER 3

Fear of The Kings

YOU FOR A VENOM SMILE

Jail mentally prison walks to your soul.
Plans of missing the love and the sudden death.
Can I reset the prison walls?
Road to success.
Road to love.
Mighty soul we come.
Too far to fall.
Alone.
Why misery loves the coming you keep.
Nowhere to go again.
Too far to fall again.
Drown in my lonely love.
No one to phantom about.
Whistle please for the love.
Sleep tight tonight all alone.
Don't run from the past.
Or taste the blood of the venom.
What I would do to feel his missing soul.
Venom is found lying in the gut of the goat.
How shall you pick that cheater behind you?
I think the numbessness.

Why Do You Think About Him?

Strife is the impurity and selfishness.
Devils will noble your abilities.
Don't get me wrong he has an intellect.
To distort your abilities.
He will start a social gathering.
In your heart.
An intoxicated guava for you to eat.
He will throw you many complaints.
Up to your malice.
He will sent sorcery to slander in the school.
He may make u think you need.
Licentious to be on the earth without marriage.
He gave you enmity to god people.

Will You Trust Him?

Dig nation to the drunkenness souls.
You feel like fear of the concrete.
With opium in the system.
Be restored to Jesus.
He's not fair to the ones who are perished.
Devils debauched like ravished people.
Don't be masquerading for the devils.
Efface him.
Or you will languish.
God's glory is like a quill.

Lucifer will deprive you from your future.
God will give bliss.

HE WAS ARE SIBLINGS

Antagonism of the world.
He has corridors for you to blaze in the lakes for the soaking of the
feet.
He will slavish the dead ones and have them
Perish the godly one.
By praying and rehearsing his chapters.
You will perilous immortal and his named in the hell.
Stop adamant the lords calling.
You think in the dig nation.
Will stop you from succedind.
You could be ministering on the earth.
Please don't be imprudent or relented.

FAVORITISM

Lucifer will send a genocide of people to the
Beseech you do not fall for the slavish ways.
Rebuke him.
Where the quadrant on the earthy.
To the demonic and the heavenly spirits.
Slander of the devils churches.
He will not have the abilities to fight you.

Back up.

I'm god I will over power the weakness.

I will make him stumble.

And fall and his sorcery do not work against me.

There fools to think he could win the battle of the kids.

I complaint my kids.

And my kids have to compliment me first I'm a jealous god.

If it is a sin for the jealous of each other belongings.

I gave them to the children.

I have the favoritism.

Lucifer does.

WASHING THE FEET

Jumping in the heart.

Cold of the fear hearing whispers.

In my soul.

He ancients and he knows.

I plead for the host.

My oppreeors love I admire.

He not ever loved before.

I choose the love he created for me.

I holocaust my footsteps behind him.

He snaked to deep in the chains.

They laughed in the disgust.

It made me grow from dust to grave.

I knew I was going to be and have a whim in all shall pass.

I don't swear I promise.

I'll be back to shine.

Standing crisp in the corner.

Whispers told me lies sold and mantles on my body they took mantles.

To see my breast and my feet.

AGGRESSIVE

Vexation me if you may.

Mufflers mantle my temple.

It will be an honor to speak to me.

Cause this day shall pass that u vexation my walk.

Whimsical men I told you.

You hurt me even if you desired me I could have pleaded to me of the beauty.

Instead you artificial gave birth.

You ashamed me.

Hung a banner across my step.

I was obedient to your words.

You will murder my appearance.

And laugh at my back.

Towards the corner.

I gave you pleasure.

You were so cruel to me.

It showed that you were just like me.

It showed that you were just like your angel.

Nothing but the broken granite of this heart.

When you told me to love you I knew that it was a game.

Is it suppose not aggressive love

It shall be come to pass.

I gave you loftiness for the child many blessings.

All I ask for your protection.

Not jealousy of my flourished.

You gave my kids offerings.

I had a faded heart of the crimson.

I wasn't ready yet to believe.

If you're caught to late you will fever the e blazing fever of the death.

I had to learn that he cared for the stressed ones.

You left me there to shell my success.

I bloom anyway to the air.

LUSTING FOR YOU

Lusting for you putrefying for the body.

Give me the pleasure while im like and granule.

We sat in the vine yards.

Together wonder about how the bodies would about

How the bodies would touch.

A Cunning mind telling me sexual figures.

Cruel beatens that's why I deservers more of than less.

I had a complex for men.

Scared to see what he felt.

Cause so many used to throw like Frisbee.

Ashamed I sat for the cherry.

Shadow shackles me in the rest.

I gave birth to marriage.

I sat down to the ointments and I seen fly's pass by threw the men fluids.

What a water dripping pleasure of the soaking together.

me and my husbad.... we had just got hitched wenty to get clothes for the kids picked up shane and then went to get it in so we launch i got to bagging on th car and all i remember was my hasband telling me he love me and it was a crash boom and i was in the back and jumped

out of shock the driver ran and the car was smash and i had to run back and grab my husband out the car. it was the day of damagage th epolice rushed killer soon ass he got ou thte car charge him wit a dui and he wasnt even driven. then took him to the hospital and he was tooken to th phsyci ward were he told them he was gone kill hiself and he called me repeaded ly and he was l;ike come down here check in so i felled bad bad and checked in wit him cause i knew he wasnt driving. so when i got there he ate my ass and it was lovely in the shower on the physi ward and then the others guys was aiming at me even staff. well they end up finding out we was husbad and wife so they moved us both,so the dope me up the whole day and staff had came and tooken my pussy and then they rape team came along and took my pants for eviedence. and the guy was try ing to beat me up ever since it happen like i usually slepp naked and i know i had to doped up and tired cause i slept in my clothes. so he came in saying what u doing want him u can do wit me and start smaking me on my asss. so i had move to get up to look around and i was move slow because of the neds he was already pulling my pants down and inserted his penis dirty staff.
Valiant self-esteem

Lattice espousal I gave supplication.
Heavy laden's made me weary.
Friends left me insight.
That I didn't need tender care.
I need just one who will always be there.
Flagons I wish to drink.
I will only get sweaty.
I need a shoulder to lean.
Instead if these shackles of the sin.
Delightful adoration.
To my face.
This is my opportunity to tell you I love you even if she there.
Take me or leave me.

Cause you didn't tell me how to go about the real selfishness of the life.
Take me or leave me.
I hope you call back.
And the love for the perspiration cause that shell come to pass.
Only in the season.

BIRTH

You shall smell the pomegranate.
Petitions I sat for the honor,
Confess that you didn't take care of my seed.
Reveal you take my toll.
Your character is funny.
Doldrums was he.
Lacking from our life so be it.
Deceiving you threw the delighted desires.
You sent me to the streets to be beat.
The last 15 minutes.
You were a reflection of me.
You made me crazy to were I could not carry on.
They flocked together to to see me fail.
That's the pretense.
I made it for being no perse.
You un pretentiously became my family not by choice.
And left me lacking in the dust.
I insiste you made birth to receive a blessing.
You stalked me then died off to the nut.

CONFESS DEATH

Artifice ur death.
Aligning your coffin.
Encouraged murder.
It was so awkward how he left.
Rhapsodoy he played while he made a riddle.
To impel at the stag night party.
Men wear blotto.
I could pellvcid.
Instead.
They broke canapé to see me dance.
The diabolical force that man gavethem.
The foulsome.
They devor me.
Like they were scounge my zit.
This was ante.
I went to anthropoid.
My soulmate didn't even ageis me instead.
He stumble to the beat.
Him and his family.

Yes man love Yes ma means agree to an higher power

Sure you commited to me.
They made sure before death.
Put mummy in that fly shet.
Foe of my love affair
Rampant to my love.
A swank to the mummy
He was homage to the streets
Behind the doors he was underneath me.

Like a luminaty is to the sky.
Multi Passover so don't cry.
Shackled in the hell.
Did he tell about the loveaffair.
Wiat your turn.
Dis complacement of the rancid.im not commited to you.
I was ill to your living.
Im gon terminate this love affair.
Wait your riddle out for the yonks.
Im still unique and full of preety amzing beauy.
You set a snare for me to move.
You knew you was an whelp of blood to my fear.
I was playing a card of the charade.
You talk like a snip at mines.
You made a howler for not marrying me.
And you otto manto relax.
Cause you are not even the blood sent to me.
Your complex was in the closet.
Next door you congradulated the queens.
Sleept with them slitenly next door.

TAKE OF URSELF

Retatiolon threw this pen.
Im a mad man to this.
Im not gon rest till this is an hailstone.
When it calms down again.
The hurricane of the desired capitol.
I leave it to the higher power.
Cause you threw with the hand of the aim of the judgement.
Cheater casket built for the lonely.

Lay I the grave for the short time of the coming.
Till phalanx comes to take you.
You will be more halcyon.
You thought u would keep a secrte about ur secret.
You called me disable.and got me sent to the stablefarmers.
I just was a perk in the shell.
You was gilt edge alone on the sid road.
Seek you ran and called brawny cousins.
What bright idea.
You exalting hima dn took his kid.
I heard dady.
Sat still.
He gave you a hearing.
You lived like feta and felt like a laughing stock.
My arms wraped around the pole.
Wher perspiring in the tomb of the beast.
Your flame was flamboyant black tee.
Need to be thrown in the fjord.
Your like a dewclaw.
I couldn't stand being yourbedfellow.
Bigcats ran us down.
They ate ur seed.
You knew you berk.
Sniffing the nightness.
They sneak down stairs at nigh to get my cake.
Hundreds of the clustered smelt your nasty gift that represented
My mate.
You put me out in the one way.
You litter ed the same skin you sex ed.
My complexion was the same and alittle lighter than yours.
You sex you rblood to let mines tempt to sex me.
You heard my cey and let it go out on e ear to another.
Cheack your backgroung before you check mine.
Eye to the blacken sparror who wouldn't fly on the leash.

You sleept wit my enimies and came back to pass the juices of the yucky scent.

You lazi man of the disgust.

Adopted flower the grew from and daisy to ad rose was me

and the lilmigent pimping you gave to her. The opium you paid her.

Mate and the blood and the grown snake.

Big cats.

Do Something You
Called The Phalanx

Coffin,coffin,creepy coffin

Fender, bender, cheaptalk.

In not a termayant im telling the truth.

This is charades cuzo.

Im here to deep for the dirndl.

The garden gave us the depression.

The fruit was biten.

He said don't eat from the middle tree.

And gave multi trees to eat.

This serpent grew crafty of the adam and eve situation.

Satan attemped to attack god.

God knew and sent him to the earth.

He deceived us like human studies of the bodies on earth.

He deceived you like that depression.

Speculations to the pride of the Christmas.

Isolation of the sonsfirst birthday the many days put out on the holidays of joy.

This the scence of the battle.

I rebuke the demonic spirits of the family curse of hatered of one another.
My breast plate is tighten up for the cusre.
The heavy loads of the passing you r child to next parent.
I reuke you from taking my seed cause you was
taking from your mother and you left me wit yours.
Lovers company in the box you put me to tell
me I was insane at the young age of the wetter trip to the goal.
This is the kigdom of the Christmas carol of the hell you pay for the curse.
A battlefield of the joining to th end.
The lake of hell.
Calling for the enimies of the heaven.
Break there faith he will not,
Fight the pwer of the demons.
Humility made me stronger.
The scence of the attudie.
You are cults to the deep dip.
Pits wont wash your feet it burn.
Temples and kneel to the lord.
The virgin cults need to go on the despot of the lord.

Feel the pain of the stomping the devils head

Equality the armorof the god.
Prptects you from the every redemption of lusifer.
I see vividly in the fortress.
Reasoning him not to battle.
Realm to realm.
Quarrel a cure in the midst of the feet.
I gave you garments and you hindrance my phone.
I fought for you with a helmant and the sword.
Held many clichés to you.
Enmesh I made you stomp for the distitions.

He put you to take avenger.
Hopley I don't fall back.
Twice I don't tell the same thing to you again.
Be and ecumber.

FITNESS FROM THE WITCHCRAFT

Money smeller like the delusion, of the
Delusion the back stabbers of thestubberness.
The druckards of the seeds.
The memory of the magic manipulation of the thought.
Eye to eye must note will dwell in the soul.
Dominating your examples of the head family.
Intimidated of the success.
The desire Of the of the fast request.
If you work you will please your maker and your flesh.
It will all be best in person.
Please don't intimidate my flesh.
Made in person.
This society tares.
The coexist with enmity to me a delusion
of the crawlers of the partakers of the gnashing acts.
priorites went last on the streets of the Lucifer.
Till the world becamedead.
Willing to fight back in the ink for what you did to me.
Tossing the fast money out and the legit money in.
And the arresting if the demon childhood took cover of the sins.
So I took over the cosmos and conceit I didn't have any sovereign
I mashed his feet in to the flames.
You was evicted at 12 to go to the devil to hurt em.

CHAPTER 4

Justice of Travail

GENES

Like problems seem not to matter or bother whats realiy
Coming to the stabbers, killers,
the sin the atomosity generation to the babies.
They shall pass through the genes.
Life problems seem not to matter.
Happiness kills the days of your life cause I feel.
Joyful passion of the feeling in my time.
Bring the war against the families.
Burning pain inside anger out my soul.
They fly out of the godly compassion.
Reality life problems.
They run threw my vains like no existing at all the crys of the blood.
Jesus brought good and bad.
People will have understanding untilthe return of the Christ itself.
Family fights and arguing and calming of the dyas.
Living the city life in the harmony.
I say beaten of the battle.
Devils it self abusement of the opium and achool.
Baet me down I say user of the understanding.
Life problems.
Seem not to matter I say I will rape you
in the night no more problems running and spitting the ballets.
like venom beat me down.
it didn't seem to matter these days.

Loveable He Is

Loveable he si its bad cach bad he is
Ran from home he did
Little did he know he was mine.
From his plea to the rain.
Foolish boy I wrote
The garden of eve.
Iknew t egood and the bad outcome of his coming
Meant for thy running to me.
Loveable he was to me.
He took me back in the justice and the labor of the clock.
Little of me you seem to wish for the trumpet to sound off early
Any day you must be ready this is not just the talk
It's the day of time to come
This is not the hypocrite its real.
System catches me in the middle of my case.
Window pain blows your mind.
Balst under the falme
The pockects of the system.
Fallen tree we ate from.
Nomore hidden suffer for along time.
Love me longtime.
Rush and be little of the plea.
Say no to me the plea.
Run from the slainful freedom.
Sent to the pain.
Pleasure stack wit me.
Soldier with me.
Captain of the love of my soul train.
Raga mugga.
Being the lust of just in me to you.

I will be spanked for my family sakes
Forsake you the time
Mission completed captured to the return.
Beat no more cuffs.
Bless me oh god.
Little oh me not the sinner of the days occasionally only

PAMPERED PARENTS WHERE ARE THY

Where are the love me not
Love me so on
Love me like a menace
Drive me away not
Leave me tampered not
Take my ring not.
Pamper me daddy so on
Pamper me mommy so on
Where must thy be with out love
Daddy don't fles
Make up to break ups
Daddy don't leave my dope
Legally prostityion occasionally cry for the babies
Sleepy train nights.
Let beat you down you left me in the room all alone
For no one to hear me
To burn the sides of the bedded
Looking froma frame
Praying I could call on the one help
Loving the older man of my dreams
That wasn't for me dragged down the floors foe my conditional lover
Left in the 15 area of the sunken days

Lasting to breath for fame
Thought I would die if I be the light of the family
Im not him,he in me yes
Let me breath imok
He called him cause he put his seed out here
It was time for him to go don't cyr
I made it ourt the glass for you
Am not the depressor.
I share the dreams of the life.
I bring the family to lesser issues.
Im the golay of this master.
Stopping all demons

REAL LOVE

They say real doest hurt so it doest suppose
To feel broken sone it will now matter
What you do or say is it back to the messages
Something nobody everknew love was compare to be for the
Time lines of the tingle in the bones.
The bump wit you was like permeable sex.
The permission was taught to you.
My love was like a rivulet
We sexed like a steeplechase and it was hale
It was like a postage mailbox shipped to me daily.
The cum of the babe.
You made me lout for your love
My bosom was like osier that swag so precisiously
I am your knew girlfriend to the end
Real love made us see the hollow ways of how much we loved each
othe

It's a wee ja without tieing the not
Otherwise you may be in the adultrss if your already token
I wouldn't take the chance
To loose you will be like the savoir cause I need an husband of true
protection
And guidance and time for me and spent pleasure of the time with
my kids.
Love was meant juat not for me and you to do unmarried.

DESIRES

Wher playing these games like where lovers.
Just like the pain so deeply care for you to cause someone
What happen to the goodies
What happen to the side of you that enjoyed
my presence what happen to that smile that took me on the sea
what happen to the face that said you wont ever leave.
you will not provde the way you suyppose to be and learn from the
my mistakes was carefully thought about being
choosen in the bed was not a choice
if you would have stayed I would not have been trapped to conceive
ilove my seed sand maybe it was a pleasure to have the m
4 get the donator o love lol
You I despise your ways of telling me to go be wit some one I dislike
Thnks for the lfe I desired to get my goals together
Yourtrash is some one else treasure
You lost my love and someone else pick me up and cleaned me
You showed me the lowest of the pit and I showed you th
Love of real pain for leaving me stranding
I chased you for the pain you put me threw

It was nt the love rtapps I couldn't stand the grin of your clownish wasy
You spoiled me wit the sluttish ways and made me think I had to work
The way I did you trick me out my mind to let someone enjoy my thongs

EMOTIONS

This is my story.
I live everything day by day
How you control whtas urs
I finally found out what I like about you go to
The roller coaster with my ups and downs you put me threw
Wit your fight ing family and there jealousy friends
The gohuse wasn't even happen
I boke all6 of yah down at on time
You could not ever feel the wrath of my body and sexually intercourse I gave you
These feelins is so strong the formats of the mental math are brains
Did to connect the adoring love you had to make me happy
The emontionals ran so deep I felt for you
You still lust ing for a man cause I was so hard
In the en d you suffer to ask me to hit nme in my donkey the devils project
This is th esulvent time of you r disgrace
You wish you could give birth with a queen
Th w closte
Is ope I don't judge I just love on this emonital roolercoaster.
Opps did I put your skim out there
The relations of the slave and the buffalo

The lighted baby maker on the one way of the corner of ne
Cant you see it I heard you sexing the queen on the celly
An dtryed to cut me off a nd blow me away for telling your histoy
The devils walls

ghost tag... well it twas the night that stole the ghostes town. and it
was a lovely
sleep. and when miralce akwaken she seen the lovely ghost of lincoln
eights she
had awaken her for miracle messing around wit floe so u know
miracle had to leave
floe alone. the ghost would come in dreams and warn her of the
guy flow and let
her see her death what had happen. so it was and shooting adead
mans body in the
middle of the street and she had crept ot the room when miralce
had awaken out
the second bed room and then she had tip toed back threw the hall
way of the first
room. so she had terrible shooken miralce but miracl wasnt really
scared she had
laid back down and went back to sleep. the ghost had wore a light
gray linen skirt
passed the knee and a white bloose and collared and when she awoke
and floe
came over in his thuggish ways mirale said what had happen. and
she scared him so
bad that she said the ghost told her to leave her alone and explained
how she had a
Checkmate boob and he said he knew exactly who she was talking
about it was a
drive by and she got killed he was messing wit her sister her name
was lisa. evry

body knew her i started to think my mind was playing tricks until more people
started to say funny stuff was happen in

check mate
I play my enimies like a game of chess.
Indistress 16 agaisnt 16
Thers one issue inthis game
You must not quit
My enimies is tamed by me
Oh this is some serious heat
My heart is beating like ragging pain for my enimies.
My Pain to let my god handle my ways of this chess game.
So now I have to thick twice of the revenge that is left in gods hands
Harder about beating around the negative bush.
Surroundings of the will I feel to end this game
me and you play entering my area
You will not win against me even how much you try
Learn to end this game
I will succed in the life cause you may always controlnothing in my
terrioty
You're the pun im the queen
You hed a nerve to think my king wanted you
I block you out and the checkmate of this lesson
I always loose the mind of the battle you think
Im sharper the the 2 edge sword
I let the others ride threw the horse man
and catch you like an L shaped and useD my castl e
to straight get at you cause you moved the wrong way
I trap you bringing you around my area
I slide to make you fear me and took ur king
leave it thehands of the higher power
Checkmate I won your mind you fear me
I sat on the stomp of the phone call

Your message didn't mean nothing to me
Cause I check you all around the board for the
56 messages you was on are wood and I still rode
You out my terrioty with my boots
I paid the most get on my level I made you trick harder to
Match my style
Check mate horror
You had foolishes ways to play wit me
Done you on yourhead game over

COMPLATIABLE

I thought we was the most complatiable couple of them all
Someone like you was broken by the law
Trance of the hymotiozer soulmate
Which one can I choose
Ladies do the picker men do the hunting
My friend indee in need, my lover in mist,
my tempted in the range of the ballad of thy dead soldier.
All we had was puppy love now its time for the big play.
From the world to love each other from the bottom to the top
Something was meant for every one to know
Planted for the jealousy you speared for me
My script is so tight I play thrace
With you r tolls you pay me for the time you talk to me
Everytime I sit back think of the time you waisted you play wit my
money
You are nit geeting away wit this time it wii; come back around
And you will pull out the dollars of the hundreds and more
Im the g of the flow of the dollas once they
transfer into my hand you have been

Deposited in to my account you thought you
played me I took all the goals
the baddest in the xcash you cant compete
wit me that's why you strip in the night cause I don't pay for anything
well taken care of by my complatable mate not
ever pulled dime out my pocket these thick lips of the
waist and the cute face of the this race Indian and black
looking like a Spanish model o n the bunny
channelthe devils mark I didn't take I prayed
and received the blessings if they was mean
t the complatiable partner was sen tfrome hell
to despise your mind and now I gone to te next watch you r
lover that sits next to you they must have a ring.

MIXED FEELINGS

I feel this way for you cause you had
differences of the way you sent the cupid from
above to love me in the hard times this is an hold-up of your heart
this is the brake up of the get back together
the channel that tilts the lining of my heart
the wind that blows my heart way far sorrow
love comes with mistakes
it also comes and goes
it shows threw mixed feelings
I have for you was mention all day in the rain
It beat lik eth e revalation
Towards the stars only one kiss matters
How is your kisses
Talkaway from th emission
Starts in th e flame I didn't fight cause I choose to be beauty

154

And you choose to be the hood of my car
The mixed feelings of the homolife
Ignore the callings of the rage
That sits in the daysod the dead daisy
You not ever had someone to treat you like rose
And then you mad for the chips you dipped in
Gameout connected by fame
You blamed me for the rush you had wit that mini feeling.
Get that prostition off your leather and them
glory boot you soak for the rest of the night for
you done for the time being.

CANDY PAINT

Tonight was the bright candy paints of the carry seed.
Make up the freezesuckers I got the paint on my hips.
Ready for the lock and load of the battle of the
return of the candypainting lords wrath agasint the devil
ready to lcok and load
follow this yellow brick raod
it leads to death of optum
side snitching lanes 4 corners of death.
The riding Beast riding charlie horse.
The demons wont play for long.
The red devil you are you leak blood.
Your wombs wont leak eternity just passing over
Freeze suckers candy paints the surrounding sweepers
Rush to the bush freeze the throne on ur face sucker

LOST SOULS

Loss soul travel the earth
Wandering from the light
Wonder how to get from purgatorty
Fighting for somelove
Hiding the darklanes
Picturing the light
Seeing the lights
Loss soulswe find
More and more show we find.
They glow.
Candle light they carry
Like the fire works
Mouth to mouth sunction
They travel the earth in packs
Like gurellias with no packs
With no sympathy.
With minds of steel plates.
Shaper than bow n arrows
Shaper than the cuts of the cracks in my heart
Loss soul travel in packs. l
The crack in my stomach
The juices of the organizations of the orgasms
This is intented in the middle of the music
The covey of the flags you hold put them down and hold the cross

STREET SWEEPERS

Swevering from side to side
Cuff to the back of the devil back
Physco what they say he flew
Biplor he sent the throne to me
To much heat from the air your
Mental disable is the devil shake heim off
Reaping pass the lights.
Flying under the cover.
The mat of the soul burning.
Almost on my toes.
Face stuck in the pillow
Scearming help to the ghost
They watch you in the night
Blowing bad thoughts to my brain
Cliff to cliff to the sea would you jump no
one will change my grave time
to the sun to the moon.
From mars to the stars
Lake to the endof the bay.
Bay to the trees.
Toy tree to the grass from the grass to the
Far away lips to the tip of the womb
My love for you is like chocolate candy
when touched it soothes my head.
Marshmellows melting from heart to smile
Like rubbing in the bed fellow
Grinding in the honey mooners den
Just to cool to have hot flashes.
Strawberries tasting like canalopes.
Put me in the mixing bowls.

Pour te honey on me from head to toe
Smack the butter cakes from side to side
My love is so coated with chocolate s honey and whip creame
Like oreos making love with thighs around your body
between ur heart to heart

CHAPTER 5

Change to Succeed

STREET TALKS

chapion ohe equerry
wicked curve of my body and soul
my everyday mundane is demolished.
You indirect object to me.
Don't walk filty side ways on me
Im gone make stitches so sick with nausea.
Im gon make you look like Neapolitan to you thieves.
You bowed down to me cause your area novice to me.
Im so nubile to the chapter.
That's why these females and males hate on me.
My heart is so numb.
These nutcases drive me in sane.
I sit back on the stoop of pressure.
Letting my temper ride off my chest like a pique of life.
Want to go to everlasting life.
Prophcying on the my life day to day sick with these thoughts
Every move I make this peopletry to chas ne with nonsense.
To ease the pain I read.
Hit the love and study the comprehension in life.
It s wrong to abide in the devils law.
The stolen goods running from the hood.
Merry pop shorty don't mistakes me as a diamond cluster machine.
Braking entering.
Tight on the matreess

Marry he replyed balcony sitting lessons learned.
On my knees to god shouting for a better day.
Mailing the postage for a beeter blessings.
Giving to the poor.
If you told you would spit tidings in your face.
Would he stab ur back.
Would you kill yourself.
Simly thoughts fo harm.
Betrayal of the hard word love.
Called by the lord the devil baiting you in
Shark attacks sinking in the trapped in a no way sitition.
I cryed allnight.
So sick with the devastion.
Crack house in the smoke room, no I didn't not ever,
Chanting with there problems yes I did.
My heart the good son,the bad son,and the ugly son.
Threating to blow my brains thedevil mention.
I dare you don't listen.
Wheres your heart mynes not beating.cars to trucks.
Hater you motive my time.
Leave me alone ill split you r heart in two just praying praying
for you.
Cause its not in my hands once you turned on me.
Release u payed police silent treatment.

MONKEY ON MY BACK

All I can do is moop.
You had that baby all I can do is mop I had 2.
You so lucky I not ever stood the ballar life.
How you get robbed for all your goods you gave it to him.

Locity is the revenge of the lord.

Me celebrate another happiness.

What a slap in the face.

Im proud for you it shows on different affects.

You sad I made you glad.

They must wasn't known about the killer rapist clown.

The demonic spirit that was in the body of his mask.

That wasn't funny you played murder and got shipped to the fire,

Play ganster and get cut off the book of life.

Inside memory mistable disagrre ment to my land.

I come to hear your quail.

Stalker so thy can hear mybones entwine.

Run, run don't let me go

You talk to me like you scared or something.

Maybe you entice me.

Back back demon.

Whom I almost thought I had a monkey on my back.

Who prayed for me.

Im running this town tonight.

Sorry for loving another man tell him.

Imscared of no man.

From my shadow was not proptected in my clothes.

We coul;d heve been like adam and eve the first to begin the earth.

For you took my kindness down the drain.

You left me for a straggler.

Knew I would want to sing some day about the times we had.

In so many ways I made you jump out ur shoes.

Realizing that you trash the opening of the mark of the beast.

Under stood this is temptation and no one forgot the ravaltion./;

The cloulds would open like a firre that can come on to me lik train
smojke.

Stay wit these people you thought had ur back its al a trap.

Take heed finish school or be homeless.

Ill meet my companion threw out the years.

You text messaging fool.
Who got the last laugh.
Brother don't trust me im the demonic an ddont mean to be.
He was this short from being a star.
Thank god you and have that monkey on your bacjk.

HOW TO GET IT

Rush money, more money, go go go
im suicidal marching in the rain
your house my manchine.
Lay low talk to me.
Stepping on my shoe.
Let it scroll off your back to the floor.
Donkey cake.
Hustling more and flowriding in on the temperature.
I sat there alnight.
Still traces of you making it known were a ganster
was popular and was noticed for his mouth and work
you queen and dike syou be homeless.
Std having for the wrong sex.
Its gon be pussing wearing the cream of the
color of the rice of many bacterias.
Don't point finger you might get robbed of all your joy from god.
Amillion times to you get the right mind set.
Straight looking for my cellypillpit for the fight ing over canteen.
We gone see share and let go and give after the battle.
Crawl on the million dallo babe.
Con gradulate your self you made you open the law of living.

Leave it alone pray.
Thousandothers who honor me shooting ink killa them threw
this ink.

ADDICTION DROP UR POST

You called me to sell priceless.
Drug addict.
I thought I was a friend of the addiction.
Rich off the night life get off the trap.
Right hand man steels your man hood.
The devil your partner ion the strre t life leave it alone.
What made you cheat you told me to.
Put the fun out your sleeve pull them up lets get money legit.
Whole hearted for the dream talking about sitting on the
porch cause you lyed about the ruff
life and put me off the porch to get the
open ing of the new defined state.
These are enough addicts put down.
Its hinder ing you you. pull threw the flaws.
The love shoot is in the past.
Remarks in the life.
Who loves me even in the even yiou wan t to be my frien d all of a
sudden.
You monk of the gold.
Phone bonnin gon the lasc day of the season.
Success my time to set the risen moon.
Not a hypocrite.
Addicts put what you think is gold down

You ate off my play on my taxes.
I approved your dish.
Your sed not ever really feed me.
My fathers death paid my daily expenses.
I look like the seed of he.
And you hate the fact that I sse the mirror.
Certain things I adore funerals I dislike.
Weapons I despise.
Passed my shoulder I conquer my fears you hinting aimer.
I proved the trails and tribulations.
I laughed in the mees of you house wife.
The wife to supply your need your money make either way.
I still brought what I had.
You got a penny put my wallet.
Did you beat my doves.
Before and after I would love to put you to death
if only you say one thing and touch my button constantly.
B stands for a beauty combnations.
I for innocent for not guilty.
Tfor the temper you put me threw
C for the crystal like glass mineral I will use to se you.
H for the habit of the trickeryyou tried to stop my success.
B*T*H means im innocent and in charge and not
guilty for for the beauty and success im in.

man where s my conflate relationship.
my meritorious man.
hes my merry making with another man.
giving me a mes caline to deceive.
Better so the one woman looks.
Would you not want to be around me no more.
The mesh I have between to og you.
The personatil thet I assume to be.
Make my so called lovers betray my touch.

Its like ive been bewithch to love my mans I feel so strongly abou t.
This is a preety theft who love you so protectly.
The look of the whole surroundings.
My palate has a lust for the two betrayers.
This man of cruel axiety.
My feet the wlak the paths of misery.
This count lesser each day of what I think
of paying another to ditch your mental downpour.
Very intellengent weapon s.
I sghall withdraw myself from the dust.
One in a cage the other in a cer.
Iwas soo to be anstonished.
I just knew to be at styate.
It was meant to survie the hardest in the battle of the fillest.
I dislike the crinmals of the association.
They have one track mionds of tempted ghoals.
The romance of the plunder of the knocking at the door.
Incouter and licensced to get it in,
A leprocard of the every night look.
My lessons in the manmchine.
The ares lil;cut in the bluinds of the window
for you under cover sleep at the house of my man.
protection managing the game so there
will be the mania of the disowned

BLAME IT

you nasty mouth whench.
grumbling old habits.
drop them for I devour you in the dust of
the mental an dreacrnate you for the ciow.

the raise fame was wanting the bottom of the
ill also tame the lonely wanting dallar I had beg
when the speard of the thought became the
attention from the guys that back down
the other girls separated my kind nee and the
weakness and I stiil blew back with the strength of the higher power.
I seen and heard all the angel and the dead raise in the next ady.
Some not know knowin ther dead.
Theuy come straight tot me.
As if thy knew that they wronged me.
They nkew that I was true and I can fell the presence so.
They see me and ask me to etll.
The alive mmore of there comin g.
And to ask for the recarnatuonof the life.
The addict of the rose.
Cheap talk of the powe of the rabbling.
To get buy buy the power of the papa joins thefreedom.
15 minutes of slients for the desied.
No on tell any thin g.
Had the world in the fending of the ghost.
Had payed the game of monopoly.
Caught the wit the cocanice hammer.
Niggas chasing by the red lights.
It fit you don't.

CONFUSED

Living wit enimies.
Pregnant by the venom man sexing by the
silibing that was like brothers confuse by
thye blood and the vane of water

that swhy my love aimed a good launcher as a child.
this cumming was like white rivers.
and death of a dead pig meats humping the video screen.
chasing the ageless child miles around the room.
listening to th hallor of the antie
the room was closed and you knew you herad
me holla r you sat there to my me hot.
so we I greew you would put me on the strip.
I was in the the line of fighter disables and the
in mty blood to do thes things I do.
1400 hundre d $ abortion AND 1400 DOLAR
FOR THE RIDER YOU SUNK MY FACE INTO A SHOTY
5 months went by you told know one of the babvy.
You put your girlon th ecke and dipped out wit m e.
Lesson of the kids.
Price was paid cause then became a queen.
Claime the arging with the brother s and the
blow you r pants off for adultrees.
He don't lik e fakery.
He saide tell you in the way you may under stand.
Massaging your are a with and transexul you will burn fo rlif e.
It is now and then.

LEARN FROM THE TEMPTATION

My ceiling like the clouds.
How beauty I watch the open sky in th room.
I lay back in th e freash past ways.
Making it righ the blues abillty of the freedome.
The wooding for the slide me across th tamper
\ wit \my hands I holla raped the m hot boys sounding for you.

The defeated grabbed the diplomas and tought
others what you know good rhythm
miracles smile what a man can make you feel.
the burn of the forgotten wipes.
what an orgasmof fame.
and you tame yourself for the pride.
the doentime of the love of the effort somebody
he got happy to lean on the ruin from the.
angry flaws not the corner of the cherished of the head ache pain s.
he no tstared wrong of the same paste.

MY BODY

Im beauty from head to toe from my eyelashes.
From my belly buttonto my eyelashes.
From my lips to my teeth.
From my curves to my mind.
From my ears to my head.
From but to my feet.
You see the flawsless compete to the thick.
To thick fortune of the breath of my feet
Walking daily on the sidelines to take over the earth.
Woman an dmen are beauty ion side and out.
Piture me rolling in the sand.
Every body looking for the same.
Everybody hating on somebody.
I see it in there eyes and heard it in there voices.
My monthly lay down.
People shouting from lane to same patse.
You not able to run wit m eim to hymtiuing to these men
Arac hood hoping the devilpour you r name from

bush to bush and disgraces you r.they so on me
they go t to take the piature causey they know theywont
succed in the getting
fall the choppers they then hit the wrong place.
crackl;ing the dresses under cover.
even the trow er walk my waist get the money of the demoni self.
you will repent once the fire blazing your last breath
it will be tlo late.

be afriend of the atick
sweet me you say I smell like strawberries.
cause you lost the money of the devils project.
to bad the panties of the hand of the sinners.
change of the no change hungry ways.
looking for the mistake.
he found the day by day shame.
tastes you syill.
She a snre of the hair and the heels of the queit euye of the chills.
One mile away get in the queit as keep the humble metaaly.
And things will go a lot easer for the long run,
Start taming the voice and steps of the labor of
the crabs you passed I didt say I had crab s I sai d you
passed it on to the burning fire of the cum.
Silly carrot I thought they said treats was for tricks.
Talk is cheap the demon only want you to treat the trick for the
Abuse and get use to the games and think you wil win
In every thing and will loose at the end.
everytghing that looks and walks pretty anit pretty.

MESSENGER

you watch the same day trying the catch the canning if you can.
I mat speak if i can,you weak speaker of the stay off the sideline.
Or get ran down and get woke up for the attention.
Circle the watch for the cucumber.
Retape the paper and get diseraspect ful
you be taped up on the wall and the shirt will say don't disturb
the rip sign and all is well left in th ehans of the beholder
we all change our ways before the last days.
to get te girl flaw offthe table you must stop putting them out ther e.
and get on ur knees to say you sorry and move over its his way now.
I tredto open the door the opened and closed.
Guess who s back I still smell the dope on your clothes
They thought they would bring me down and they lied on the fact
of life.
They hid the terror from society.
My feelings of the laughter of hurt.

Miracle ps.they raped me and charged me with charges that wasn't
True and I had to plead guiltyfor lesser time my family set me up
and my xfriends
You would think blood is thicker then water and water is thicker
then blood for more
Stoires buy this book and your family is your worst enemy and the
devil takes
Takes advandtage don't let them. take your mind rebuke the demons
they had money and
Set me up cause they had money and thought they ran the city they
didn't want me

to brake the family curse of not the mother not taking care of there own child and
sending them to other relatives I refuse im gone fight for mines left in gods hands.

I

ABOUT THE AUTHOR

Cheetah Diamond, I am an African American writer who participated in various school extra cirriculum activities, such as: soccer, basketball, and swim team. I was a flag girl too. My dream was always to follow my poetry life and to become a cosmotologist. I graduated from cosmotology school and still I write my poetry. My favorite pets are dogs. I am married at the age of 26 years old. I have 3 lovely children. Here I am today, inspired to write my first book "Decieved was the Trait of Love"

Printed in the United States
By Bookmasters